BUILD A GOLDEN BRIDGE

BUILD
A GOLDEN
BRIDGE

How to Lead Change
When You're Not in Charge

MICHELLE PAUK

PONTE
PRESS

PONTE
PRESS

Published by Ponte Press
www.streamsidecoaching.com

E-book ISBN: 979-8-9929414-2-5
Paperback ISBN: 979-8-9929414-1-8
Hardcover ISBN: 979-8-9929414-0-1

Printed in the United States of America

First Edition, 2025

Cover Design
Elisabeth Heissler Design
www.ehgraphicdesign.co.uk

Interior Design and Typesetting
Elisabeth Heissler Design
www.ehgraphicdesign.co.uk

Copyediting by Liz Wheeler

Author Photograph © Tausha Dickinson

For Derik, Ingrid, and Owen,
and all my many teachers

Table of Contents

List of Illustrations

Introduction

When were you last asked to make a significant change at work? Perhaps you had to adapt to a new organizational structure or a new boss. Maybe you needed to start using a new tool or comply with a new corporate policy. The change might have included several of these things. It could have affected your life outside of work, too.

What was your initial reaction to the news? You might have wondered why the change was necessary or felt frustrated or angry that no one consulted you. Those feelings may have faded quickly, or they could have hardened into resistance or cynicism over time.

It would not be unusual if you reacted negatively. Few of us eagerly act on changes we did not initiate, yet this is how most organizations expect people to respond. The change demands are relentless, and there is never enough time to address everyone's feelings or ask for their opinions. So they write an email, make an announcement at a town hall meeting, and hope everyone will go along and do as they are told.

Just one question. How is that working?

If your organization is anything like most modern corporations, dealing with change leaves much to be desired. Over the last twenty years, I have felt this way as an employee affected by change and a change agent in various companies, ranging from small startups to Fortune 100s. A recurring theme in these experiences is how often leaders attempt to reduce the inherent complexity of transformational change by focusing solely on what they can predict and quantify.

The typical approach is to develop plans to mobilize the

change *en masse* by relying on management principles for achieving economies of scale. We streamline the change process for efficiency and then determine a timeline for execution. We then follow the plan despite objections and declare the change "successful" upon completing the prescribed change activities. Rarely do we examine whether the intended behavioral and business outcomes have been achieved; often, they have not.

The problem with this plan-driven approach is that most organizational change is far messier than any plan could anticipate. Change necessarily creates uncertainty. It is impossible to predict how the change will unfold or plan all the moves required to arrive at the desired destination successfully. When we focus only on the plan, we willfully ignore reality and hurt our chances of success.

Uncertainty about change is inevitable, but it is not the primary source of the difficulty we experience while navigating it. The primary cause of our suffering derives from gaps in awareness, empathy, and communication throughout the change process. If we attend to our experience of change and respond thoughtfully as new information emerges, successful outcomes are far more likely. We simply need to bridge the gaps. This book will show you how.

WHO THIS BOOK IS FOR

If you are in the middle of an organizational change and wish the process could be better, this book is for you. This book is for change leaders at all levels, especially those lacking positional authority who must use influence to get things done.

Middle managers—team leaders, project managers, and process improvement experts—are at the heart of most organizational change. Senior leaders expect them to deliver on the change objectives, while employees expect them to resolve the problems that arise during implementation. Mid-level leaders also bear the emotional burden of the change most heavily. They see the personal cost for employees and empathize with their struggles, yet they often feel they lack the power to improve the situation.

If you find yourself in this position, how you choose to navigate the change process will tremendously impact those affected by the change and the broader outcomes for the organization. You have far more power and influence than you may realize. This book will show you how to put the influence you already have to good use.

The concepts and methods will be equally helpful if you are a leader with positional authority. They are particularly relevant for managing resistance or influencing peers outside your control. No matter where you are in the organizational hierarchy, you can use these ideas to make a real difference in the experience of those around you and improve outcomes for your organization.

HOW TO USE THIS BOOK

In the following pages, you will learn how to improve the experience of workplace change using straightforward approaches you can put into practice immediately.

We will explore the impact of seven common skill gaps in organizational change and how to build bridges across them to enhance your effectiveness as a change leader:

Self-awareness

How to increase your self-awareness so your behavior doesn't unintentionally undermine the change effort.

Empathy

How to inspire others to change through empathy and connection so that you can preserve morale and trust.

Effective conversations about change

How to enhance your communication with deeper listening so you can build relationships and understanding.

Engaging with resistance

How to productively leverage resistance, complaints, and doubts to build momentum.

Context sharing

How to create a shared context for the change that aligns interests and motivates collective action.

Securing leadership support

How to gain the leadership support and resources needed to ensure the change is successful.

Personal resilience

How to stay flexible and grounded in uncertainty and handle setbacks more calmly and confidently.

Each chapter contains three key elements: core ideas drawn from psychology and behavioral science, real-world scenarios to illustrate the concepts, and practical tools and templates to help you put these ideas into practice.

I have included several anecdotes based on my experiences as a change agent and executive coach to provide a real-world context for these ideas. I have changed the names and other identifying details to protect my clients' and colleagues' privacy. These stories represent real-life experiences, but the particulars presented here do not depict specific individuals or organizations.

I have also included several templates you can use to organize your thoughts as you apply these ideas to your work situation. You can access downloadable copies of these resources on my website, www.streamsidecoaching.com. These resources form a ready-to-use toolkit you can apply in various change contexts.

This book is organized in a natural progression of concepts, with each skill building on the previous. Applying the ideas in sequence will help you maximize your results.

In Chapter One, we examine the impact of our self-awareness on others, including how our willingness to listen influences others' openness to change. Chapters Two and Three provide a framework for facilitating change in one-on-one conversations with empathy and effective dialogue. Chapter Four will show you how to use these strategies to engage productively with resistance. In Chapter Five, we examine techniques to create a shared context for change. Chapter Six explains how to secure the necessary leadership support and resources to ensure the success of your change effort. In Chapter Seven, we reflect on the experience of leading change and the opportunities it provides for growth and personal resilience in the face of uncertainty.

If you are new to facilitating change or find yourself leading without authority for the first time, you will find it helpful to read the chapters sequentially, as each concept builds upon the previous one. If you are an experienced change agent or leader looking for additional methods to add to your repertoire, you may prefer to treat this book as a reference, with each chapter providing a set of patterns for a particular context.

Facilitating change at work is not simple or easy. However, it can be much better than it is today in many organizations. Change does not need to be painful—not for you or anyone else. It does not have to come from the top to succeed. Workplace change can be respectful, humane, and successful, and you can lead the way.

1

Self-Awareness

When I was promoted to project manager in my mid-twenties, my colleagues at the software company where I had worked for a few years as a content developer congratulated me by saying, "Welcome to The Dark Side."

I knew what they meant. Our company's project managers had a reputation for being hard-nosed about business. They got things done and were not afraid to employ a range of Machiavellian tactics to guarantee success.

I did not welcome the conversion. I wanted the job because I believed I could do things better than my project management peers. I understood the content developers' needs and wanted to use my new project management role to make everyone's lives easier. It did not take long, though, before I succumbed to the seductive pull of The Dark Side.

I lacked positional authority. Except for a few short-term contractors, the people on my project teams did not report to me. I quickly learned that I could not make anyone do anything. I could, however, make it very uncomfortable for them *not* to comply with my directions.

My methods were crude and often brutish. A clipboard with a checklist was a favorite device:

"Can I have an update?"

"Is it done yet?"

"When will you be finished?"

"This is past due."

When this tactic failed, it was time to use heavier artillery: public embarrassment at the weekly status meeting or a fiery email to the underperforming person's manager.

It worked for a time. I didn't make many friends, but I did get things done. One colleague told his peers I was "a bloodhound," which I took as a compliment.

And then, something shifted. Like many people who undergo a transformational change, I did not arrive at the idea alone. Instead, external circumstances forced me to find a different way.

In my second year as a project manager, I was assigned to work on a very complex new product. My role was to project manage content development while the software development work was simultaneously underway. Three content teams, consisting of approximately forty staff members and two dozen contracted voice actors, were included in my scope. In addition to managing the timeline and dependencies among these teams, I liaised between the content development department and the software development teams developing the new product.

Things quickly became overwhelming. I realized that my methods for managing my simpler projects would be woefully inadequate for this new challenge. Although I knew I didn't have time to checklist everyone to death, I was unsure what to do instead.

At one particularly low point, I got into a shouting match at a weekly status meeting with the manager of a content team for missing a key deadline. When I asked for an updated date, he refused to answer. "We've never done this before," he protested. "We can't possibly guarantee when we'll be done."

"Unacceptable!" I snapped.

You can imagine how the rest of the meeting went.

Sometime after this exchange, I realized how ridiculous I had been. My reaction nearly ensured this man would not return to another status meeting or be honest with me about his team's progress. And while it was aggravating to leave a question mark where a revised date was supposed to go, it was nonetheless the most honest answer to the question.

In the following weeks and months, I had a change of heart. I wish this transformation had been purely the result of introspective reflection. Instead, a more pragmatic dilemma made me realize I needed to change my approach. I was pregnant with my first child and would soon be going on maternity leave.

As I prepared for my leave, I had to face the facts of my impending absence. Things would go on without me. My ego would not have permitted this admission before, but my fast-approaching parenting duties required me to accept the obvious. I could not manage things by simply putting in more time. I had to find another way, one that required much less of my involvement.

So, I began experimenting with new ways of accomplishing my objectives. Instead of personally tracking progress and endlessly torturing a Gantt chart into submission when things went off-track, I shared the bigger picture with my project team. I showed them how their work connected and how delays in one area would impact other tasks.

And then I stepped back.

Our weekly progress meetings shifted from the harsh interrogations I had relied on to maintain order to a more dynamic and egalitarian conversation. I knew something remarkable had happened when one of the content team producers shared news about a delay and immediately explained how he had coordinated with two other teams to ensure the overall schedule would stay on track.

This was a clear sign of success for me. I finally realized that my task had not been to "manage" all the work and harass the team to keep things on track; instead, it had been to set up a structure and environment so that everyone could manage the work themselves.

ACKNOWLEDGING THE INNER TYRANT

What does this story have to do with facilitating change? What is most important about this is not how the story ended but how it began.

I do not consider myself a tyrant, yet I know I possess all the necessary qualities and skills to make other people miserable when I am stressed. Many of us share these traits under the right (or wrong) conditions.

Before attempting to engage with others to understand their views about change, we must confront our own. In this chapter, we will examine our motivations as we facilitate change and explore ways to keep our needs in balance with those we serve. Understanding and attending to these needs is essential as we develop our capacity and willingness to listen to what others may find difficult to share.

As a project manager, I made my work and countless others' more difficult because I personalized anything that went wrong as a reflection of my competence. If something failed to go according to plan, this was an indictment of my poor planning ability. I had internalized the regrettable notion common to many of these roles: mine was "the one throat to choke." Consequently, any bad news was intolerable, and I would punish anyone who brought it to me.

Unfortunately, most of us have worked with or for someone with little tolerance for bad news, criticism, or negative feedback. Popular management culture normalizes these behaviors with sayings like "Don't bring me problems—bring me solutions!" It is easy to recognize how damaging this attitude can be in others; often, it is much harder to recognize these patterns and beliefs operating within ourselves.

Acknowledging one's inner tyrant is the first step in unwinding this thinking and associated behavior. When does your inner tyrant show up? What does it want you to believe about success and failure? What is it attempting to prevent by suppressing bad news?

ACTION AND REACTION

With my coaching clients, I often use a reflection exercise to help them identify what is at the heart of the tyrant's behavior. I call this the *Action/Reaction Sequence,* shown in Figure 1.

The Action/Reaction Sequence is based on a principle I have observed in many change contexts that mirrors the dynamics conveyed by Newton's third law of motion: for every action, there is an equal and opposite reaction.

The reflection sequence is as follows. Consider a situation where you have been frustrated by another's unwillingness to change or comply with a request. Now, ask yourself:

- What am I feeling?
- What am I thinking?
- What is at stake for me in this?

Now, consider the other person. Ask yourself:

- What might be at stake for them?
- What might they be thinking?
- What might they be feeling?

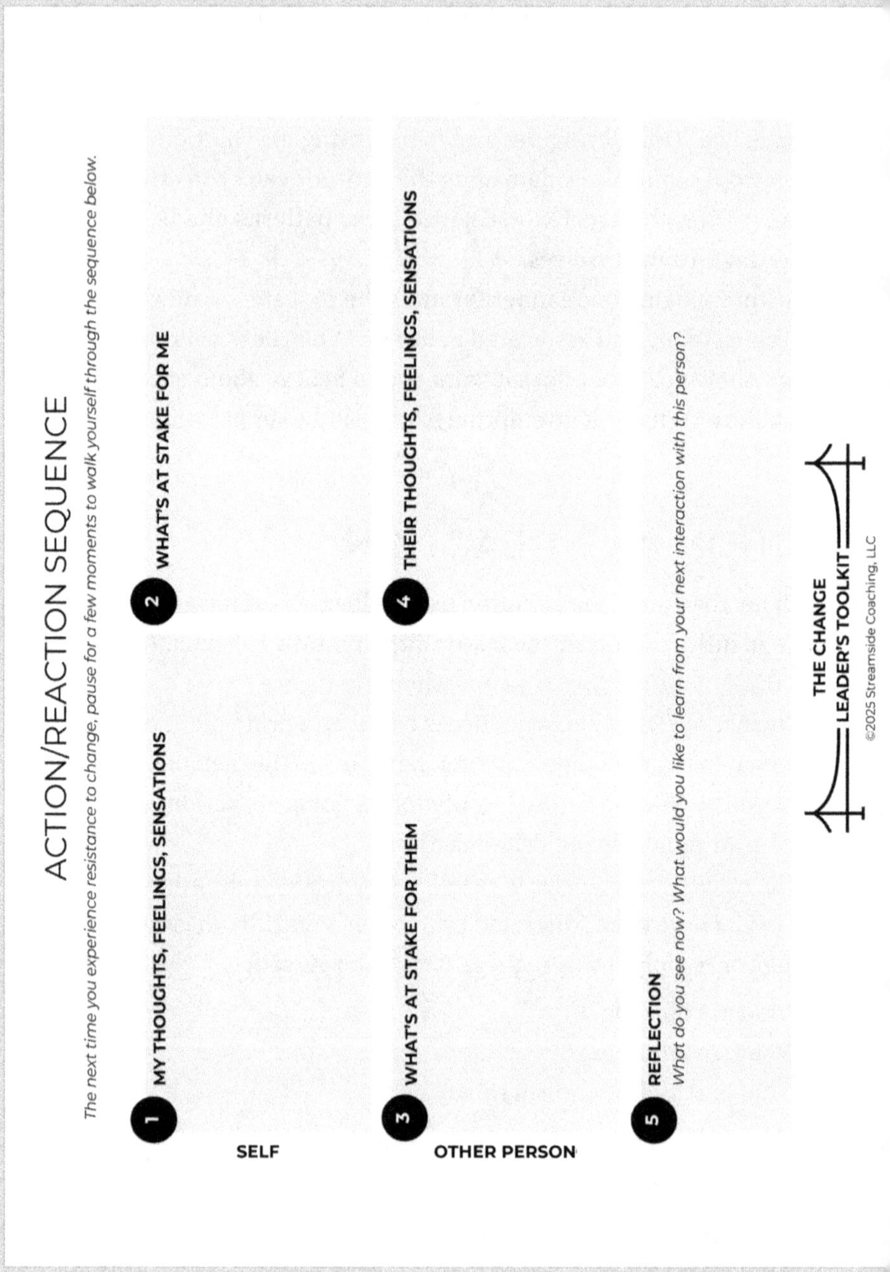

ACTION/REACTION SEQUENCE

The next time you experience resistance to change, pause for a few moments to walk yourself through the sequence below.

SELF

1 MY THOUGHTS, FEELINGS, SENSATIONS

2 WHAT'S AT STAKE FOR ME

OTHER PERSON

3 WHAT'S AT STAKE FOR THEM

4 THEIR THOUGHTS, FEELINGS, SENSATIONS

5 REFLECTION
What do you see now? What would you like to learn from your next interaction with this person?

THE CHANGE
LEADER'S TOOLKIT

©2025 Streamside Coaching, LLC

Figure 1 The Action/Reaction Sequence

Walking through this reflective exercise reveals an unsettling mirror image for most people. The more important the issue is for you, the more important it will likely be for the other person. Interestingly, the things we are concerned about—typically our success and our reputation—are what we realize are also at stake for others.

If I had reflected on these prompts following my heated exchange with the content team manager, I probably would have come up with the following observations:

What am I thinking?
"I need to make sure we stay on track. How can I do that when I don't know when they'll be done?"

What am I feeling?
Frustrated. Stressed. Under a lot of pressure.

What's at stake for me?
My reputation as a project manager. Maybe our ability to deliver the project successfully—what if we can't get things back on schedule?

What's at stake for him?
Strained relationships with his staff if he pushes too hard. Lost credibility with leaders if they can't deliver. He might be worried about his job.

What might he be thinking?
"We've never done this before. We wish we knew how long it would take, but we don't know."

What might he be feeling?
Frustrated. Stressed. Annoyed. Probably also under a lot of pressure.

Had I stepped back to examine the situation this way, I would have seen that the heat in our conversation came from our *shared* concerns and fears, not because we were on opposite sides of an argument. Although we had different perspectives and areas of focus, we were both stressed about navigating an uncertain situation and worried about how this would affect our roles.

Gaining this awareness is a powerful way to build empathy, but I encourage you to take this reflection even further. As organizational psychologist Kurt Lewin observed many years ago, behavior is a function of the person and their environment (1936). What environmental factors may influence your perception of what is at stake? What assumptions might you be making? What else could be true—for you and them?

When you discover something important to you by reflecting in this way, it is often easier to turn toward more productive, solution-focused thinking. Consider how you would like to engage with this person differently. What thoughts, beliefs, or assumptions would naturally lead to the kind of interactions or relationships you prefer? What would be the first sign that your working relationship had improved?

DESIGNING AN ENVIRONMENT TO BRING OUT YOUR BEST

My inner tyrant thrives on the desire for control and perfectionism, two of my most deep-seated character flaws. I was drawn to project management because I am an excellent planner. I like plans because they help me feel in control.

The problem with being an excellent planner is that I am utterly lost when something does *not* go according to plan. Perfectionism then prevents me from moving forward productively. I stew over what I perceive to be an error in my planning and become paralyzed. This can become highly problematic when leading change; when we attempt something new, we will encounter much more that we don't know than what we can safely anticipate in a carefully constructed plan.

Left unchecked, my control and perfectionist impulses spill

over and contaminate my interactions with others. They manifest in various counterproductive leadership behaviors. In addition to the previously mentioned checklist harassment, I can be inflexible and close-minded. I might refuse to delegate or slip into micromanagement. I can become so concerned about doing things "the right way" (my way) that I push others aside and do not notice or appreciate their contributions. These behaviors interfere with my ability to lead change humanely and effectively by cutting off my empathy, patience, and the ability to listen.

Do you recognize any of these tendencies in yourself? If so, consider when they appear. What environment draws out your inner tyrant? What keeps it in check? As I have observed these patterns in myself, I have also learned what kinds of work environments tend to call forward my most unpleasant traits and which ones bring out my best. For the last decade, I have been drawn to work in Agile environments because they offer productive and systematic ways of handling uncertainty. With Agile methods, we keep our plans light and focused on the next right thing to do. We plan to re-plan; the structure is inherently flexible. By experiencing the benefits of teamwork, experimentation, and iterative learning in Agile contexts, I have developed a complementary skill set that serves as a counterweight to my inner tyrant. Most of the time now, I can keep the tyrant's worst traits safely at bay.

ROUTINES FOR MAINTAINING BALANCE

Part of what makes this relatively easy now are the routines I have established over the years to keep myself balanced. I used to think these routines were merely nice to have, maybe even self-indulgent. Now, I see them as essential for maintaining a balanced perspective. Keeping myself grounded is a prerequisite for making a positive impact on others. Without intentional focus, it is easy to regress into thoughtless behaviors that undermine my purpose.

For instance, the direct relationship between my state of mind and my ability to serve comes into sharp relief when coaching one-on-one. If I have not tended to my routines, I am easily distracted by my thoughts in the conversation. My mind wanders to my to-do list, assorted worries, and other mundane preoccupations. The lapse is noticeable to the other person. In the most benign form, my questions lack focus, and my reflections lack insight. In the worst case, I dispense unwanted advice, derail the conversation in long-winded detours about my experiences, or become judgmental when I need to show empathy. To do my job well, my first order of business is to take care of myself.

If you lead others—whether with authority or without—you have this obligation to tend to your well-being. Many leaders I coach feel guilty about claiming even small snippets of time for themselves. They have become habituated to running from meeting to meeting with scarcely time to catch their breaths, let alone take reasonable breaks or ensure they have had proper rest, nutrition, and exercise to fuel their best performance. If you have previously brushed this off as unimportant or considered it "selfish" to prioritize your needs, it is time to take another look.

To examine this more closely, open your calendar and look at the last week. First, notice how many scheduled meetings or activities you had. How many hours were you double- or triple-booked? Next, notice how much free time you had. Did you have room to take breaks, eat lunch, and focus on your most important work? Did you have time to be creative, playful, or even slightly bored?

Creating intentional free space is essential to becoming a more effective change leader and facilitator. You will need this space to regulate your emotional response when challenged by resistance or difficult feedback and to find creative, collaborative solutions to complex problems. If you know what routines help you be successful and simply have trouble finding time to practice them, you are not alone. Many things can throw us off balance: an illness, travel, or changes in responsibilities at home or work, among others. Continue practicing. Perfection is not required.

MAKING A POSITIVE IMPACT STARTS WITH YOU

If you haven't found a set of daily habits or routines to stay balanced and grounded, try experimenting with positive psychology principles to foster flourishing and well-being. The past two decades of research in positive psychology have yielded a wealth of practical and effective interventions that you can use to enhance your enjoyment of daily life and your sense of satisfaction from eudaimonic pursuits. Some of the most effective practices, such as maintaining a daily gratitude journal, require only a few minutes of your time each day.

When I was having a particularly challenging time at work a few years ago, I began studying positive psychology and experimenting with various evidence-based practices to improve my outlook. For example, my day often started with meetings I did not enjoy. Consequently, I would wake up with dread, and this feeling would linger into the afternoon and evening. To combat this effect, I began experimenting with intentionally devoting the first part of my day to creating positive emotions. Before logging on to my calls for the morning, I would spend ten minutes playing piano, reading poetry, or meditating.

The effect was surprising and asymmetrical. Even a very short investment of time in the morning doing something I loved had positive effects that lasted well into the day. Staying focused, remaining calm, and engaging in creative problem-solving were easier. As this experiment illustrates, dedicating time to one's well-being need not be onerous or taxing. Even small investments can yield beneficial results.

In addition to intentionally curating activities that elicit good feelings, there are other ways to bolster your well-being. Here are some habits that have been particularly helpful for me. Some of these may resonate with you.

Habit 1 » Start the day with something you love.
Spend ten to twenty minutes before your first meeting doing something that brings you joy. Try meditating, playing music, dancing, or journaling. See what happens when you bring these good feelings into your first call.

Habit 2 » Measure success by your true purpose.
Pay more attention to what is meaningful to you about your work than outside measures of success. What is your true purpose? What tells you that you are working in alignment with your purpose? My true purpose is to serve others with empathy and connection, so I focus on listening deeply to my clients and creating spaces where they feel seen and heard.

Habit 3 » Keep experimenting.
When you feel stuck, try something new. Read and talk to others for fresh ideas. When we experiment and explore, we learn and grow.

Habit 4 » Cultivate appreciative awareness.
If we slow down long enough to notice, there is almost always more going right than wrong. What can you appreciate about life today? How does that influence your mood? What can you help others notice?

Habit 5 » Create community wherever you go.
Prioritize individuals and interactions (my fellow Agile practitioners know this well). Offer to help others and find

ways to let others use their talents to help you. We all love to feel useful and appreciated. We will be rewarded in kind when we are generous with our smiles, laughter, and time.

Of course, the habits that will work best for you may vary from those I shared. Dedicate time to experiment with different approaches, and pay attention to what lights you up and refreshes your spirit throughout the day.

As you do this, remember that this self-discovery work should be a joyful pursuit. I have made the mistake of trying to manage myself too strictly with these routines and have gotten depressed and discouraged when I realize I have not taken the time to meditate, go for a run, or connect with a friend. Instead of measuring yourself, try creating what author Emily Ladau calls "F.U.N. goals" for your well-being habits and routines. These goals should be flexible, uplifting, and numberless. What a freeing idea for the perfectionists among us! Go on and give it a try.

IN SUMMARY

In this chapter, we have begun to examine how our willingness to listen can influence others' willingness to change. Our presence has a tremendous impact on those around us, particularly those we lead. If we wish to make a positive impact on others and facilitate change humanely and respectfully, we must begin by recognizing our capacity to harm, even unintentionally.

Begin by noticing when you feel pressure to succeed, especially when your success depends on another person's actions. Instead of transferring the pressure you feel to others, find ways to alleviate the stress. If you can do this proactively through regular routines, balance will be much easier to maintain.

Marcus Aurelius, Roman emperor and Stoic philosopher, wrote in his *Meditations*, "the mind converts and changes every hindrance to its activity into an aid; and so that which is a hindrance is made a furtherance to an act; and that which is an obstacle on the road helps us on this road" (1882). This ancient wisdom applies to what we can learn as we navigate change and lead others through it. The problems we encounter point the way to the solutions we must find. If we are too short on time to listen to our thoughts, we will never be able to truly listen to what others try to share with us. Once we commit to resolving this impediment, we will be ready to move on to the next.

2

Empathy

When the Agile transformation started, Dana was one of the first project managers to volunteer as a scrum master. She was enthusiastic about her work, but her methods were idiosyncratic and often ineffective. She also developed a reputation for ignoring feedback, preferring her unique approaches to industry-standard methods. After a year or so, Dana's boss assigned her to work with one of my fellow Agile coaches to bring her in line. It had not gone well.

My manager asked me to coach Dana and told me this was a last resort. If Dana did not change her behavior after coaching, she would be forced to return to her former project management role.

I did not fully appreciate what I was getting into. It soon became clear that Dana did not want coaching, and this quickly became a miserable experience for both of us.

Each week, we would meet for thirty minutes in the office cafeteria. Dana would open her laptop, bring up the team's task board, and launch into a twenty-nine-minute monologue about the team's progress and tasks without pausing for breath.

I listened on high alert, crouched like a lion in the long grass. When Dana finally stopped talking, I would pounce, pelting her with "helpful" comments and "powerful" questions such as these:

"The Scrum Guide says..."
"That might work, but it's not best practice."
"Have you thought about trying this instead?"
"Don't you think it would be more effective if...?"

Then time was up. Dana would snap her laptop shut, and that was it.

Unsurprisingly, Dana's work showed little improvement with my "coaching." As the weeks passed, I became convinced I was failing my task because she refused to budge.

So, I tried being more forceful. I would cram in some unsolicited advice about what Dana should do differently. I would argue directly, point for point, with her approach.

Still, nothing changed.

Then, one day, a tiny thought crept into my mind a few minutes before our meeting: "I wonder how Dana feels about this."

I realized then that I had broken a cardinal rule about helping others. In college, I participated in a peer writing tutor program where we learned how to coach fellow students to improve their academic writing. A key mantra was this: "Coach the person, not the paper." The whole time I worked with Dana, I was coaching "the paper"—the task board, the process rules, the backlog. I had completely ignored the person sitting in front of me.

When Dana sat down for our next meeting, I took a deep breath and asked her if I could start with something I wanted to say. She nodded, surprised. I said, "Dana, I want to apologize to you. I've realized that this whole time we've been working together, I haven't been listening. I've been trying to force my ideas on you, and I haven't even bothered to ask if you're interested in hearing them. I'd like to change that today. Would that be okay with you?"

Dana's shoulders relaxed, and a wide grin slowly spread across her face. She offered me her outstretched hand. "Thank you," she said as we shook hands. "This has been the best session yet."

Dana never became a model scrum master, but she did keep her job. Our conversations got better, too. It took continued discipline on my part not to interrupt her to inject my views, but I made a conscious effort to listen first and be judicious about what feedback I chose to share. Dana put in extra effort as well. She kept meeting me each week and gradually started asking my opinion and considering my advice. We learned from each other through the process—something I never thought possible when we started.

WHEN WE HAVE SOMETHING TO PROVE

Working with Dana taught me some extremely valuable lessons about the roles we play when we facilitate change. I accepted the task without acknowledging my feelings about the assignment or considering how that might influence our interaction. Had I taken some time to reflect on this, I would have noticed an internal conflict: a sense of pride at being chosen for a challenging task, a desire to prove myself capable of helping this person, and sincere doubt that I would succeed.

One factor contributing to my self-doubt was a strongly held assumption that Dana would resist working with me. Before I went to meet with her, I would prepare myself for battle. I figured it would be a blow to her ego to be assigned to work with me, mainly because of our surface-level differences: I was much younger and new to the company. Without any evidence supporting my assumptions, I was convinced Dana would dismiss me as someone with little to teach her. As if to impress on her that I did have something to share, I went into our conversations more forcefully than I needed to. I was trying to prove something, mostly to myself.

I also felt I had something to prove to my leaders. I wanted to show that I could be effective as an Agile coach. They had made it clear to me that this was Dana's last chance. I hoped the coaching would help Dana be successful for her own sake, but even more so, I wanted her to be successful for mine. If I could "save" Dana from the brink, especially when others had tried before and failed, this would demonstrate my value as a coach. At least, that is what my ego wanted me to believe.

This is some very complicated psychological territory. I had positioned myself as both Dana's adversary and her rescuer. Neither of these roles was appropriate for the relationship or the task. How can you possibly help someone when you are fighting them at the same time? The combative posture I instinctively assumed heightened the emotional stakes in our interactions. Had I been better attuned to my emotional climate, I would have had room to be more curious about Dana's experience and support her as a peer.

Perhaps you can recognize some of your own interactions in the dynamics of my relationship with Dana. Maybe you have experienced internal conflicts while facilitating change or felt you had something important to prove while helping others. This chapter will examine how our unspoken and often unconscious attitudes affect our ability to facilitate change with individuals. We will also explore moving beyond these automatic and reactive postures by cultivating intentional curiosity and empathy while working one-on-one.

THE ROLES WE PLAY

In the 1960s, psychiatrist Eric Berne developed a theory called transactional analysis that explains the pattern of interaction we see demonstrated in my experience with Dana. According to the theory, we each possess three "ego states," systems of feelings and corresponding behaviors. The three primary ego states are Parent, Adult, and Child. Ego states include patterns of self-talk, beliefs, and behavior we have internalized as the result of past experiences (Hicks 2017). These patterns are deeply ingrained and usually operate automatically without our awareness.

Each ego state serves an important function. Briefly summarized, here are the core functions of each ego state (Hicks 2017):

Parent ego state
    The "Parent" holds the rules we have been taught explicitly and implicitly throughout childhood from our parents and other parental figures. The Parent holds our ideas about how we *should* behave and helps us navigate the world with healthy limits and boundaries.

Adult ego state
    The "Adult" evaluates information objectively and makes rational, balanced choices based on what is appropriate for the present context.

Child ego state
    The "Child" responds emotionally to events like we did as children. The Child ego state holds our playfulness, creativity, and spontaneity; it also helps us to comply appropriately with expectations and social norms.

The Parent and Child ego states are grounded in past experiences, while the Adult ego state is rooted in the present. With the guidance of the "integrating Adult" ego state, all three ego states work together to help us navigate our environment and social interactions successfully.

Most of the time, the feeling and behavior patterns governed by our ego states are helpful. Sometimes, however, they can be counterproductive and can negatively affect our interactions with others. Under stress, the Parent and Child ego states can both become "contaminated" by irrational or inflexible thinking patterns that create unhealthy dependencies (Hicks 2017). For example, the contaminated Parent ego state may take the form of a rescuing parent who swoops in to save a helpless child or a critical parent who criticizes and reprimands a child for disobedience. The contaminated Child ego state may take the form of a compliant child (*"Just tell me what to do."*) or a rebellious child who flouts authority (*"You can't make me!"*).

Interestingly, the ego states we assume in our language and behavior can evoke different responses in those we interact with. Imagine you made a mistake at work, and your boss calls you into her office. She asks pointedly, just as a critical parent might: "What on earth were you thinking?"

What is the immediate reaction that pops into your mind? For many people, this kind of interaction will trigger a response from a contaminated Child ego state. You might rebel inwardly or outwardly or immediately concede fault and feel ashamed. These almost instantaneous responses give us good reason to be thoughtful with our language in stressful situations; we can easily invite unproductive interactions if we are not mindful of our word choice and tone.

Understood in this light, it is little wonder Dana responded to my coaching attempts as one might expect a defiant, rebellious child to behave. I approached Dana with my critical Parent ego state on full display by constantly harping on the "rules" and telling her what she *should* be doing. If I had approached Dana from my Adult ego state, our conversations would have been quite different. Instead of arguing over the rules, we would have focused on examining the facts of the situation and finding reasonable options for moving forward.

CHOOSING YOUR ROLE

Leaders with positional authority are often counseled not to rely solely on their position to influence others. Most people can easily understand this: very few enjoy being told what to do. Even though we might comply with an order from a controlling boss, this behavior rarely wins our respect, loyalty, or enthusiastic participation.

If you are not in a formal position of power, you might assume you are exempt from worrying about abusing your authority in your interactions with others. As I shared in the story about my work with Dana, the fact that we were peers in the organizational hierarchy did not prevent my inner tyrant from coming forward in our interactions. Although I was junior to Dana in many respects, I nonetheless assumed the role of a critical Parent when I tried to help her by stressing "the rules" and insisting she follow them.

When we recognize these internal dynamics, we create space to tap into our agency and choose how we want to show up. The most productive conversations come from Adult-to-Adult communication. This interaction is balanced, rational, and grounded in the present situation. I can share my view with you, and you can share yours with me. We will both leave the conversation with a richer mutual understanding.

In his book *Humble Inquiry*, Edgar Schein describes the attitude needed to facilitate balanced conversations, even when significant differences in status, authority, and power are at play. Schein defines Humble Inquiry thus: "*Humble Inquiry* is the fine art of drawing someone out, of asking questions to which you do not already know the answer, of building a relationship based on curiosity and interest in the other person" (2013). This attitude is essential for producing the kinds of relationships that move things forward.

We are more likely to adopt such an attitude when we realize we must depend on the other person to achieve our goals. Schein refers to this as "here-and-now humility" (2013). If you are in a helping or facilitative role, such as a team coach or project manager, your success depends on the willing participation of the people you serve. Similarly, if you are working on a cross-functional team or negotiating with peers to accomplish a complex initiative, your success is interdependent with the success of others. This is also true when you are the boss—if your staff refuses to follow your instructions, you will not be successful either. As Schein explains:

> This kind of humility is easy to see and feel when you are the subordinate...because the situation you are in defines relative status. It is less visible in a team among peers, and it is often totally invisible to the boss who may assume that the formal power granted by the position itself will guarantee the performance of the subordinate. (2013, p. 12)

When we fail to acknowledge our "temporary dependency" (Schein 2013) on the other person, we inhibit open communication in our interactions. This lack of acknowledgment is part of the dynamic I experienced with Dana. I was dependent on Dana's willing cooperation to achieve my goal of helping her. Because I failed to recognize this, we made no progress. The dynamic only changed when I purposefully humbled myself by apologizing to her. The apology returned us to more equal footing and allowed us to see how we could benefit from working together.

LEVERAGING CURIOSITY TO DEVELOP YOUR EMPATHY

Curiosity and empathy are central to cultivating an attitude of Humble Inquiry. Curiosity and empathy require temporarily suspending what you know or assume to uncover another person's perspective. Many people confuse empathy with *psychologizing*: explaining another's behavior by making assumptions about their mental state or background. For example, my early assumptions about Dana included psychologizing about our generational differences and how that might affect her openness to taking advice from a more junior person. Rarely is this kind of thinking helpful for creating a genuine, respectful connection with the other person. We might believe we understand why someone acts the way they do based on this kind of speculation and theorizing, and this often prevents us from remaining open and curious about their experience.

Empathizing requires us to adopt the other person's perspective—to see what they see and feel what they feel. One way to develop greater empathy is to use an Empathy Map, a tool commonly used in user experience and design research. It is also helpful for change agents and leaders who need to influence others, particularly when we perceive that they may resist the change we want to implement.

THE EMPATHY MAP

OBSERVATIONS

BEHAVIOR
Observable actions or inaction

LANGUAGE
Word choice

NON-VERBAL CUES
Body language, tone, & energy

INFERENCES

EMPATHIC INFERENCES
Reasonable explanations for response

POSSIBLE THREATS/REWARDS
What could be gained or lost?

LIKELY CHANGE STANCE
Moving things forward, along for the ride, or maintaining the status quo?

**THE CHANGE
LEADER'S TOOLKIT**
©2025 Streamside Coaching, LLC

Figure 2   The Empathy Map worksheet

THE EMPATHY MAP

The next time you experience resistance, try noting what you observe on the Empathy Map template (Figure 2).

The top row of the Empathy Map is for observations. These are the things you notice when interacting with the person. As you record your observations, do your best to stick to the facts without attributing a judgment or explanation.

There are some practical techniques that will help you fill in an Empathy Map:

Behavior

Notice what the person is doing and also not doing. When do these behaviors occur? Do you notice any patterns or contradictions?

Language

What do you notice about the person's word choice? Are there particular words that they use frequently? How often do they use positive or negative emotion words?

Non-verbal cues

What do you observe about the person's body language, tone of voice, and energy? Are there any mismatches between their words and the tone or energy displayed?

Before moving on to the next step, review your list. Are your notes based on observable facts, as a journalist might report? Remove any assumptions or biases from your notes if you find them. Take a few minutes to let your observations sink in. For example, if you note that the person hunches over in meetings with a frown, assume this posture for a moment. What emotions and sensations emerge as you sit hunched over with a frown?

Now, we will infer what this person might feel, think, or perceive in this situation. The bottom row of the Empathy Map provides prompts for inferences.

Empathic inferences

What would lead a reasonable, responsible person to have this response? What empathic inferences can you make?

Possible threats and rewards

What might the person stand to lose or gain in this situation?

Likely change stance

What stance has this person likely taken regarding the change? Are they moving things forward, simply along for the ride, or working to maintain the status quo?

An empathic inference, while still a guess about another person's behavior, differs from an assumption in one key respect: it attributes the cause of the behavior as a reasonable response to an external situation rather than a defect or fault inherent in the person. For example, imagine that someone has just cut you off in traffic. What would cause a reasonable, responsible person to do something this rude and dangerous? Perhaps they are rushing to the hospital after learning that a loved one was injured. Maybe they had to swerve unexpectedly to avoid debris in the road. It could be that they simply did not see you. You need not concoct an elaborate story to develop an empathic inference. You are simply making a generously minded guess about what might be happening—the kind of guess you would hope others would make about you when your behavior is less than ideal.

As you develop your empathic inferences, consider how the person might respond to potential threats or rewards presented by the change. The introduction of a new tool can mean someone who has been an expert finds himself suddenly a novice. Reorganizing a department may separate colleagues who are close friends. Policy changes can threaten our autonomy or undermine our sense of fairness. When we see we have something to lose as a result of the change, we'll do our best to avoid it. By contrast, when there are potential rewards, people are more likely to embrace change and move forward.

Lastly, consider what role you believe the person has chosen concerning the change. With any change, there will be a relatively small percentage of people who enthusiastically push forward, a majority who simply go along, and another small percentage who resist. Those who resist often have something important to say. In my experience, resistance rarely indicates the person is stubborn, lazy, or stuck in their ways. Instead, it is a sign that the person has a different perspective and may see something we have not noticed.

After you have finished recording your notes in the inference section, review the entire map. What picture emerges about this person? For many people, working through this exercise casts the "difficult" person in an entirely different light. Although we may still not share their perspectives or agree with their conclusions, we may suddenly find ourselves able to appreciate something new about their situation. In Figure 3, you can see an example of a filled-in Empathy Map.

When we cultivate empathy through genuine curiosity, we take the first critical step toward creating positive change together. However, we must remember this is only the first step; many more follow. After you have completed the Empathy Map exercise, the next step is to talk one-on-one with the person to confirm and deepen your understanding of their perspective. The next chapter will share a conversational framework designed for this purpose.

THE EMPATHY MAP

NAME Dana   **DATE** November 14

OBSERVATIONS

BEHAVIOR
Observable actions or inaction

Attends weekly coaching meeting

Focuses on team's task board

Doesn't implement advice given

LANGUAGE
Word choice

Talks frequently about team motivation

Says "this is working for us" in response to feedback

NON-VERBAL CUES
Body language, tone, & energy

Avoids eye contact

Shoulders hunched over

Speaks rapidly without pausing for breath

Appears frustrated when offered advice

INFERENCES

EMPATHIC INFERENCES
Reasonable explanations for response

Might feel things are going well and don't need to be improved

Might be upset or offended by being told to work with a coach

POSSIBLE THREATS/REWARDS
What could be gained or lost?

Status: Dana had a solid reputation as a project manager; she probably wants to maintain this in her scrum master role

Autonomy: Wants to do things her own way and rely on her experience

LIKELY CHANGE STANCE
Moving things forward, along for the ride, or maintaining the status quo?

Dana wants to be an effective scrum master (in this way she's moving things forward) and she wants to do things her own way (in this way she wants to maintain the status quo).

THE CHANGE LEADER'S TOOLKIT
©2025 Streamside Coaching, LLC

Figure 3 An example of the Empathy Map worksheet for my client, Dana

IN SUMMARY

Thoughtful change facilitators approach their interactions with others as peers. Instead of telling, they listen; instead of forcing their perspective, they remain curious about the other person's point of view. These change agents are patient, knowing that sharing ideas rarely does any good unless the other person is willing to hear them.

This is not easy, especially when the stakes are high, and you have something to prove. One of the core difficulties in navigating such exchanges is maintaining the ability to hold your perspective while simultaneously seeking to understand another's. If you feel uncomfortable in the process, this is a good sign that you are stretching in the right direction.

3

Effective Conversations About Change

Ineffective conversations about change often feel like a bad sales pitch. If you are on the receiving end, you will doubtless find yourself bored or annoyed by a long list of reasons why other people find the change compelling, only to be pressured to commit to "buy-in" at the end. If you push back, you will probably get the hard sell, maybe even laced with a threat about going to your boss or some other unpleasantness (a checklist, perhaps?) designed to coerce you into compliance.

How will you feel when the conversation finally, mercifully, ends? Most likely, you will leave this exchange with bad feelings. First, you will not be fond of the person selling you the change and will probably do your best to avoid them in the future. Second, you will not be any more inclined to go along with the change—in fact, the conversation may have hardened your resolve to oppose it.

If these tactics are ineffective in producing the desired result, why do we resort to them? One reason is a mistaken belief that they produce results more quickly than taking the time to understand people's objections and address them thoughtfully. You may make some initial progress this way, but this approach will undermine your initiative's long-term success. Another simple reason I believe many people resort to these methods is that this is the only way we have ever experienced organizational change.

The Bridge-Building Conversational Framework offers a more humane and respectful way to bring about workplace change. Applying the framework is simple, requiring little more than patience, self-discipline, and thoughtful preparation. This chapter will explain how to use this approach to improve your one-on-one and group conversations about change.

THE BRIDGE-BUILDING FRAMEWORK FOR ONE-ON-ONE CONVERSATIONS

Bridge-building conversations have three key elements: curious intention, appreciative listening, and actionable reflection. *Curious intention* begins with your preparation for the conversation as you consider what you would like to learn from speaking with this person. The meeting agenda and purpose should demonstrate openness and communicate your interest in the other person's experience. *Appreciative listening* creates space for honest dialogue by treating the speaker respectfully, even if you disagree with their views. *Actionable reflection* after the conversation encourages you to use what you have learned to build your relationship with the person and adapt your next steps based on your new insights.

The following steps will help you implement these ideas. Use this checklist as a guide for each stage of the conversation process.

» HOW TO PREPARE

Set your intention for the meeting.
Before scheduling the meeting, take time to consider what the most important thing to accomplish is in this conversation. What do you hope each of you will leave with? What do you hope to learn?

Set the stage by clearly stating your purpose in the invite.
In your meeting invite, include a clear description of what you would like to accomplish in the conversation so that the other person has time to prepare their thoughts before the meeting.

Prepare a few open-ended questions in advance.
What would you like to learn about this person and their perspective? Review your list and make sure they are questions you do not already know the answer to. Do not use disingenuous questions to force your point of view (e.g., "Haven't you thought about..." or "Wouldn't it be better if...?").

Clear your mind before you join the call.
Give yourself a few minutes before the meeting to pause your notifications, reflect on your intention for the call, and take a few deep breaths to center yourself.

» HOW TO BEGIN THE CONVERSATION

Thank the other person for joining.
Begin the call by thanking the person for taking the time to meet with you. Express your interest in learning about their perspective.

Share your goals for the conversation and invite the other person to share theirs.
Briefly share what you hope to accomplish in the conversation and which topics you want to address. Ask the other person if there are any topics they would like to discuss and incorporate these into your agenda.

» DURING THE CONVERSATION

Focus your attention on listening to understand.
This is harder than it sounds. Many of us naturally listen to respond instead of listening to understand. If you listen to respond, you are busy formulating what you will say while the other person is talking. Your mind should be clear and open while you listen. Listening this way may make you uncomfortable, especially when the speaker pauses. It becomes easier with practice.

Reflect back what you hear.
Confirm your understanding by reflecting back what you have just heard. Do not worry if there is something you misunderstood. The other person will clarify if you have gotten something wrong. This is also helpful when you are unsure what to ask next—it will give you more time to think about where to take the conversation.

Share your views and ask for their reaction.
It is possible to disagree without making the other person "wrong." When you share your views, frame them as your opinion rather than the truth. Follow up by asking for their thoughts and listening carefully to how they respond.

» WRAPPING UP

Thank the other person for their time and for sharing their views.

You can elaborate on this by noting what you learned from the conversation and how this will help you.

Be especially kind to those who have shared difficult feedback with you.

Thank the person for sharing as sincerely as possible, even if you are the target of the criticism. It is never easy to hear harsh criticisms and complaints, but they provide vital information you need to be successful. For each person who verbalizes negative feedback, several more have the same perspective and choose to remain silent. The ones who share are your helpers. Treat them with gratitude and respect.

Briefly explain what you plan to do next based on what you have heard.

If you can commit to a particular action, do so and make sure you follow through. If you are collecting a variety of viewpoints to inform your next steps, share how this conversation has helped you in the process and what the result will likely be.

» AFTER THE CONVERSATION

Reflect on how the conversation felt and what you might try next time.

Were there any points when you felt triggered, defensive, or emotional? How easy or difficult was it to listen to understand? Note any new insights you have gained about the person and their perspective, and consider what else you would like to know. What learning will you bring forward into your next conversation and your next steps?

BRIDGE-BUILDING CONVERSATIONS IN GROUP SETTINGS

Defensiveness is one of the most significant barriers to open, honest dialogue. The Bridge-Building Conversational Framework is effective because it emphasizes respectful listening to reduce defensiveness on both sides. In group settings, you can apply these same principles to defuse tension and create inviting spaces for authentic dialogue about change among many people with different points of view.

Another key consideration in groups is how to reduce the natural anxiety present in conversations about change. If we can minimize potential anxiety in the environment, we make it easier for people to navigate the anxiety caused by the uncertainty about change. Possible sources of environmental anxiety include losing face in front of others, feeling coerced into participating, being isolated from friends or peer groups, or being mistreated (e.g., being minimized, interrupted, or shut down).

To alleviate potential stress from these factors, I follow a few principles when facilitating events and designing conversational forums about change:

Principle 1 》 *Make it voluntary.*

Explicitly label learning events as optional and use the language of invitation when writing meeting requests, even when attendance is expected. People are more likely to participate and engage when they feel it's a choice. You can amplify this sense of choice at the beginning of the meeting by asking participants to consider what they would like to get out of the time they are investing. You could structure this as a silent reflection in a large group or webinar setting or a round-robin discussion in a more intimate small group workshop.

Principle 2 >> *Make it welcoming.*

A straightforward way to do this is to greet each person by name as they join. In a large webinar, you can ask participants to put their names or other information in the chat and read comments aloud (e.g., "Hello to Meg from Tampa!"). For a large, in-person group, introduce yourself as people enter the room to establish early rapport. Thank the group for choosing to spend their time with you and their fellow participants.

Principle 3 >> *Provide multiple acceptable ways to participate.*

Active participation and engagement can look very different from person to person. Some will be eager to speak in front of a large group, while others will prefer to reflect on their own in writing. Well-designed, inviting spaces allow people to engage in the ways best suited to them without penalizing them for opting out of an activity that would make them uncomfortable.

Principle 4 >> *Use intentional facilitation structures to surface as many points of view as possible.*

Make room for quieter voices by incorporating opportunities to express ideas in writing. In a smaller workshop, you can ask participants to respond to a prompt on sticky notes or a digital whiteboard before opening a discussion on the topic. For large events, try polling software like Menti or Poll Everywhere to gather input from the crowd. To surface multiple voices in conversation, use facilitation devices such as round-robin or popcorn sharing (one person speaks and then chooses the next person to speak) in smaller groups. In large groups, try Liberating Structures such as 1-2-4-All (Liberating Structures 2024).

Principle 5 >> *Honor all contributions (especially those you personally disagree with).*

If you create an inviting space to generate interest and enthusiasm in your change effort, you must ensure everyone feels welcome. This means maintaining a neutral stance in your facilitation and accepting all contributions from participants, even if you disagree with them. Arguing openly with someone to prove a point in front of a group only alienates others and discourages people from speaking their minds.

BEGIN WITH APPRECIATION

One of my favorite ways to create inviting spaces for dialogue about change is to begin with Appreciative Inquiry-inspired exercises in the place of traditional icebreakers. David Cooperrider developed Appreciative Inquiry in the 1980s as a strengths-based approach to organizational change (Orem et al. 2007). Instead of diagnosing problems in the system, an Appreciative Inquiry practitioner seeks out what is already working well and helps the organization discover how they might amplify these strengths.

I have used an Appreciative Inquiry-inspired exercise for two years to open an annual leadership retreat for nonprofit leaders. At the beginning of the session, I ask the participants to pair up with one other person and share a story about their best experience volunteering with the nonprofit organization. As they listen to each other, they inquire about what made the experience such a highlight and what conditions allowed the experience to emerge. At the end of the twenty minutes, everyone is smiling. Some look relaxed, others excited. They are all energized by their passion for their work together, and many are surprised by the depth of what they have learned about each other in this short exercise.

I choose to begin with this exercise because it grounds the group in their shared dedication to the organization. It also reminds them of what is possible when they are working at their best. When we move into more challenging topics later in the day—for instance, what changes they need to make to work well as a team—having a clear sense of their best and highest purpose is a touchstone.

NOT MAKING OTHERS WRONG

The other beautiful thing about beginning with appreciation is that it provides ample room for discovery without making anyone wrong. Making people wrong, whether implicitly or explicitly, is a decidedly poor way to encourage them to engage in a change process. Often, this happens inadvertently, as in a mandatory training program that educates participants on the new and "correct" way of doing things.

During one corporate Agile transformation I participated in, we invested significant time and effort in mandatory training early on. Some people found the training valuable and were open to our ideas, while others were hostile and resentful.

At the time, I had a hard time understanding the negative reaction, but retrospectively, it seems perfectly logical. As Edgar Schein succinctly put it, "Once you've established your attitudes about work and life, you don't particularly want to change them. It's just not a joyful process to give up your values and beliefs" (Coutu 2002).[1] As Agile coaches, we expected the people we trained to be as enthusiastic about Agile as we were. But why should they be? We were asking them to abandon the methods that had worked for them in the past. No wonder they sometimes did not receive our message with open arms!

---

1 From *Harvard Business Review*, "The Anxiety of Learning" by Diane Coutu. Published March 2002. Copyright © 2002 Harvard Business School Publishing Corporation. Excerpt reprinted with permission of the publisher.

IN SUMMARY

Thoughtful, respectful conversations are the simplest way to build the necessary bridges to navigate the difficulties of change. By remaining open and curious throughout the process, you will build trust while gaining important information about the other person's perspective.

Your ability to regulate your emotional response, especially when faced with criticism or strong disagreement, is essential for these conversations. Take adequate time to prepare ahead of time and reflect afterward. As you continue to practice, these skills will become more natural and fluid. They will be essential for engaging productively with resistance, which is the focus of the next chapter.

4

Engaging with Resistance

I spent most of my thirties working as an Agile coach and scrum master in various companies, from smaller startups to multinational corporations. For years, the most frustrating part of my job was resistance to change.

Take, for instance, my experience with Naveen, the CTO of a tech startup that a larger company had recently acquired. Naveen had hired me as a contract Agile coach to help his team adopt Agile ways of working as they prepared to integrate into the technology department of the larger firm. It was my first Agile coaching role, and I was very excited to share all the wonderful things I had learned about Agile methodologies with Naveen and his team.

Naveen had always been a hands-on technical leader. He had written most of the codebase and worked with the same core group of developers for years, including at other companies he had co-founded and successfully sold.

I remember explaining to Naveen in an early team meeting that he was not technically on the scrum team and would not be welcome at certain meetings. His eyes nearly popped out of the sockets, and veins started bulging from his neck and forehead. This was his team, after all! He saw no reason not to attend their meetings, and he was not about to accept my pronouncements about self-organizing teams as a justification.

Naveen tested all of my rules about what good scrum looked like. He wanted to attend the team's retrospectives (a usual no-no for the boss). He pushed back when a vendor team wanted to implement continuous integration and deployment; he wanted to continue to sign off on each release personally. We clashed regularly as the team learned more about Agile and encountered some of the more radical ideas, such as self-managing teams or pair programming.

At the time, I thought my job was to enlighten Naveen and protect the team from his interference. I had almost lost sight of the fact that Naveen had hired me and that he had done this quite purposefully. He wanted his team to be successful as they navigated the merger. Naveen had an equal, if not greater, interest in helping his team succeed with the changes—the stakes were just as significant for him as they were for me.

In time, I realized that it is highly counterproductive to label behavior like Naveen's as "resistance." Naveen offered me *vital information* about the environment in which we were working. We never know how the organization will respond when introducing a change from outside. Resistance, especially vocal resistance, provides the first clues about what we must address for the change to be successful in this specific environment.

Many people view resistance in a negative light. They see complaints, pushback, or noncompliance as a problem to be solved, squashed, or swept away. They see resistance as interference with the change. I have learned to see it as something else entirely. Resistance is the first sign that the idea of change has made contact with the on-the-ground reality. It means we are gaining *traction*.

RESISTANCE AS TRACTION

Traction is essential for forward momentum. When a new idea makes contact with an existing environment, friction is a natural result. Just as car tires on an icy surface slip and spin without moving forward, a change idea is an abstraction that will not gain momentum until it makes contact with something solid on the ground. The friction is necessary to pull forward.

As I experienced with Naveen and his team, friction was one of the first things we encountered when we tried to apply Agile concepts to their work. This should not have been surprising or alarming. Quite the opposite—it was a sign that we were making progress.

The family therapist Virginia Satir explains this phenomenon with her well-known Satir Change Model (Satir et al. 1991), shown in Figure 4. After the introduction of a change, resistance is the immediate next step. We push against the change as we work to understand if the change is needed and how it will affect us. As we work through this push-and-pull process, we experience what Satir labels the "chaos" phase. Eventually, we enter the "transformation" phase that allows us to integrate the change into our experience. After a practice phase in which we strengthen the new learning, we arrive at a new status quo and achieve higher levels of performance.

The chaos phase can be alarming because it is unclear how things will turn out while we navigate through it. We do not have the vantage point of the transformation to reassure us of

THE SATIR CHANGE MODEL

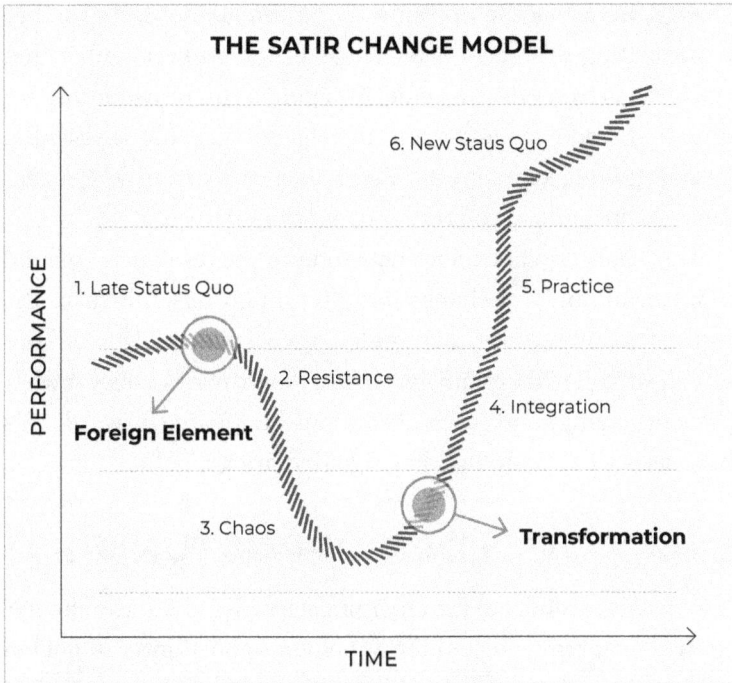

Figure 4 The Satir Change Model, from *The Satir Model: Family Therapy and Beyond*, by Virginia Satir, John Banmen, Jane Gerber, and Maria Gomori. Reproduced with permission of John Banmen.

our eventual success. If we are leading others through a change process we have previously navigated ourselves, we might lose patience at this point. Because we have already walked this path, we may be overly confident that we understand what the experience will be like for others. We might have forgotten what it was like to be uncomfortable or uncertain during the process. As a result, our curiosity atrophies, and our empathy withers. We wonder what is taking so long!

But as Satir's model shows, resistance is not a permanent state. It is a point in time in a longer change process. Losing our patience and resorting to force or coercion to accelerate the change often has the opposite of the intended effect. The key to navigating this stage as a change leader is to remember that your role is to serve as a guide. As a guide, you provide support, direction, and encouragement to keep going. What is essential is maintaining momentum. Resistance as traction keeps that momentum going if you respond to it productively.

This chapter will explore how to leverage resistance to build momentum for your change initiative. In groups, this takes the form of seizing what I call "golden opportunities." For one-on-one settings, I will explain how to use resistance to uncover what prevents change and co-create options for moving forward. This process is what I call "building a golden bridge."

SEIZING GOLDEN OPPORTUNITIES

If we listen carefully to the emerging narrative about the change, we will eventually encounter a "golden opportunity." A golden opportunity is a chance to address a concern, complaint, or doubt about the change in a way that builds rather than inhibits forward momentum.

Many change leaders become concerned that someone complaining about the change in a public forum could undermine the initiative and encourage others to resist the effort. I believe that the complaint is not what undermines the change—it is the leader's response. All changes will have detractors, many of whom have valid concerns. If we minimize or sideline these concerns, we lose credibility with the person who has raised the issue and anyone who observes the exchange.

Most of us have learned that it is wise to ask for feedback at some point when introducing an idea. Fewer of us are prepared to receive that feedback, especially if it is negative. When we ask for input and immediately dismiss it or label it as "unconstructive," we reduce the likelihood that we will receive other feedback in the future. This might benefit our egos in the short term, but it rarely helps us lead effective change.

The natural consequence of responding poorly to negative feedback is that people stop sharing their views. When we do not hear anything specific that indicates otherwise, it can be tempting to conclude that the plan is acceptable to everyone involved. "Silence is consent," as I have heard many a meeting facilitator declare. Silence, though, can mean many things. For instance, it might mean any of the following:

- *"I'm confused. I'm afraid I'll look dumb if I ask a question."*
- *"I disagree, but I've learned there's no point in arguing."*
- *"I'm frustrated. I've tried to share my opinion before, but no one has listened."*
- *"I'm disengaged. I'm not paying attention to this conversation."*

We cannot confidently conclude that silence means consent or anything listed above. Our best strategy is to encourage dialogue—even if it is uncomfortable or unpleasant.

THE LIGHTHOUSE METAPHOR

Encouraging dialogue is easier to say than do in practice, especially when facing a strong critique of something important to you. To help with this, I use a metaphor to reframe how we think about resistance. Imagine we are on a boat, sailing toward the change. Some of us will be rowers; we want to move the change ahead. Most of us will be passengers, content to go along. Some of us will be anchors; we are settled in the status quo and want to keep the boat in place. And others of us will be lighthouse keepers, warning about potential hazards in the path ahead.

We tend to misunderstand the lighthouse keepers' motives. We might assume they are trying to stop progress, but instead, they are trying to prevent disaster. They see something hidden from the rowers' view.

If you consider resistance this way, the complaint or doubt raised is no longer an impediment to forward progress; instead, it is a beacon pointing out a hazard in the path. With the hazard illuminated, you have a golden opportunity to address it and clear the path forward.

RESPONDING TO RESISTANCE PRODUCTIVELY

To take advantage of a golden opportunity, you must first demonstrate that you recognize and appreciate the gift you have just been offered. For this reason, when someone complains or points out an issue in a workshop or training I am leading, I pause and thank them sincerely for raising their concern. Others often share the sentiment but simply have not been vocal about it. By receiving the concern with genuine appreciation, you demonstrate your willingness to hear how the change is perceived and find mutually agreeable solutions for moving forward.

Some leaders find dealing with open dissent or disagreement difficult because they feel pressured to resolve the issue immediately. This is not usually necessary. Most of the time, you can acknowledge the point and commit to following up with the person in a later conversation to understand the issue thoroughly and develop options for a resolution.

Of course, your credibility depends on your follow-through. The next time you meet with the group, mention the concern and explain how you have addressed it. Thank the person again for bringing this item to your attention so that you could improve it. If you remain consistent in nurturing the feedback loop in this way, you will find that resistance naturally converts into forward momentum.

Sometimes, it is necessary to address an issue when it surfaces. I find this happens most frequently when I facilitate teams that need to reach a consensus on an important issue. Rather than pressuring the dissenter to concede, I invite the team to examine the situation from the dissenter's perspective. What new information have they brought to light? What would need to change for the dissenter to support the decision? How would the team like to proceed? Rather than deciding how to move forward, let the answers emerge from the team whenever possible.

BUILDING A GOLDEN BRIDGE

In my training classes and group coaching programs, I teach a conversational framework for productively addressing resistance in one-on-one conversations called *Building a Golden Bridge*. The inspiration for this exercise comes from the wisdom of ancient Chinese military strategist Sun Tzu, who counseled, "Build your opponent a golden bridge to retreat across." If you have cornered an adversary into a position from which there is no escape, you should fully expect that they will fight you with all their force, resulting in catastrophic losses on both sides. The wise general provides his opponent a way to escape without losing face—a golden bridge.

In the context of facilitating organizational change, building a golden bridge allows everyone to save face as we look for mutually acceptable options for moving forward. By "everyone," I do not simply mean the person resisting the change; I also mean you. If we are not open to changing our minds in light of new information or negotiating for a mutually acceptable solution in good faith, we cut off the possibility of building a golden bridge. If you feel emotionally triggered by the situation, take a few minutes before approaching the other person to work through the Action/Reaction Sequence in Chapter One.

When you have acknowledged what is at stake for you about the change and are relaxed enough to be genuinely curious about the other person's point of view, you are ready to engage in a bridge-building conversation. There are a few key principles to keep in mind.

Principle 1 » *Motivation is a function of confidence and importance.*

We are motivated to change only when we believe it is important and we are confident we can successfully implement it. If we are unsure if the change is worth our time and energy or if we doubt our ability to be successful, we will find reasons to delay moving forward.

Principle 2 » *We always have choices.*

Even if the change is "mandatory," the person still has a choice: whether or not to comply. Resistance is one way people exercise their autonomy. If you try to limit autonomy—especially if you do not have the authority to do so—expect to amplify resistance. By contrast, when we feel at choice in our decision to change, we are much more likely to move forward productively and use our internal resources to work through obstacles we encounter.

Principle 3 » *All choices have consequences.*

A fundamental rule of human behavior is that we cannot control other people's actions. All actions and choices, however, have natural consequences. When someone takes an impassioned stand on a particular issue, they have not always considered the consequences that may accompany their position. In some cases, refusal to comply with an organizational change may result in disciplinary action or termination. It may mean a loss of respect, status, or group membership. We need not frame these consequences as threats; asking what is likely to happen is usually sufficient to reveal the impact of a given choice.

Principle 4 » *Don't sell. Let them tell you why they need to change.*

We are much more likely to change when we have articulated our reasons for change rather than accepting someone else's. To illustrate this, consider two different sales experiences. In the first scenario, a pushy salesperson inundates you with reasons to buy a particular product and pressures you for the sale. In the second, you select a product with the help of a salesperson who answers your questions without pressuring you one way or another. Most of us would prefer the second scenario. The artful change agent helps people select an appropriate path of their own volition.

STRENGTHENING MOTIVATION TO CHANGE

My thinking about bridge-building conversations derives from motivational interviewing techniques, which I learned during my executive coach training at the University of Texas at Dallas in an excellent course taught by Professional Certified Coach Meg Rentschler. William R. Miller and Stephen Rollnick developed motivational interviewing in the 1980s for use in therapeutic settings. Motivational interviewing helps others change by activating their internal motivation and helping them identify the resources and options they have for moving forward. In organizational change, we can use these techniques to support others to change in a way that respects their autonomy and agency.

To support others in strengthening their motivation for change, we need to tune our listening for subtle signs of openness to change, also known as "change talk" (Miller and Rollnick 2013). Change talk indicates the person's awareness of the need or desire to change. It can also signal the person's belief in their ability to change or their commitment or readiness to move forward. Here are some examples of what change talk sounds like across these categories:

- *Awareness:* I should, It's important
- *Desire:* I want, I'd like to
- *Ability:* I can, I know how
- *Commitment:* I will, I'm going to
- *Readiness:* I'm ready, I'm prepared

We can help others identify and strengthen their reasons for changing by responding positively to change talk in a bridge-building conversation. One of the core motivational interviewing techniques that helps with this is using a combination of inquiry and reflective listening skills, summarized by the acronym OARS: asking open questions, affirming, reflecting, and summarizing (Miller and Rollnick 2013).

Open questions invite the person to elaborate on their thinking. Some powerful directions for elaborating on change talk include discrepancy, looking back, and looking forward. *Discrepancy* questions can be used to interrupt conversations that become stuck, with a participant focusing only on problems. You can interject solutions-focused contrasting questions into this cycle of problem talk like "What would you like instead?" or "How would you like things to be different?" *Looking back* encourages the person to recall past successes, which can be a great source of confidence and provide ideas for moving forward in new situations (e.g., "When have you successfully gone through a change like this before?"). *Looking forward* asks the person to envision the future and consider what might happen with or without the change; for example, "Imagine it's a year from now. What would be different for you if you successfully made this change?"

Affirming highlights the positive, a key part of approaching the other person with empathy. Affirmation must be genuine and respectful to be effective. It should be focused on the other person and not come from the Parent ego state in the form of praise or judgment (for more on ego states, revisit Chapter Two). You can affirm by reflecting back when you hear the other person say something positive. For example, "You enjoy your work as a business analyst" or "You know how to get things done with the current way of working."

You might hesitate to affirm anything positive you hear that does not align with the direction of the change. I encourage you to listen first with empathy and focus on affirming the *person* independent of their views on the change. When you demonstrate that you can notice and appreciate what is working well about the current situation from their perspective, you show that you are open to learning about the person's experience. Affirming builds trust and mutual positive regard.

Reflecting is sharing what you have heard the other person say. Reflecting is an art that does not come naturally to many people. It requires practice and experimentation to learn to do it well. Many people attempt to reflect by simply parroting what the other person said. It quickly becomes irritating if the reflection is too rigid or too frequent. Artful reflection honors the essence of what the person has said. It also allows the person to hear their thoughts in a new way. This experience is what makes reflecting so powerful for amplifying change talk.

Two reflection techniques are particularly valuable in bridge-building conversations. The first is a simple reflection. In a simple reflection, you use the other person's language to share what you have heard. It is important to stay neutral; do not inject emotion words that the person has not used. For example, "I have so much going on right now" could be reflected as "You have a lot going on at the moment." We would *not* want to reflect such a statement with an emotional label, such as "You're feeling overwhelmed," because it may trigger a defensive emotional response that will re-entrench the problem.

The second reflection technique is the double-sided reflection. Use this technique to respond to statements of ambivalence, such as "I want to be a team player, but I don't see how I can manage this new effort with my current workload." To reflect this statement, replace "but" with "and." For instance, "You want to be a team player, and you don't know how to manage the new effort with your current workload."

The effect is subtle and powerful. The word "but" reinforces ambivalence by framing the problem as two opposing conditions, so the person remains stuck. By replacing "but" with "and," we recast the problem into two conditions that must be satisfied to find an acceptable solution. This new framing activates our problem-solving mindset and encourages us to look for possible solutions.

Summarizing is the final conversational technique borrowed from motivational interviewing. It is a form of reflection that succinctly paraphrases the other person's speech. Summarizing is especially effective when the person has shared a lot of information about what they are thinking or feeling about the problem. By summarizing, we help the person distill a swirl of thoughts into the core issues they can act on.

THE GOLDEN BRIDGE WORKSHEET

You can use the Golden Bridge worksheet (Figure 5) to help you put these principles into practice.

Next, we'll go through the worksheet in detail, covering some possible approaches to filling it in.

» TOP ROW UNDERSTANDING RESISTANCE

The top row of the worksheet focuses on understanding resistance. When you inquire about the other person's perspective, do not attempt to persuade, convince, or influence them in any way. Instead, focus on learning more about their experience from a curious, empathetic perspective.

Current situation

Record any *objective facts* about the situation. Some questions to uncover facts about the current situation include the following:

- How do things work now?
- What is your role in the process?

THE GOLDEN BRIDGE WORKSHEET

CURRENT SITUATION
Objective facts

PROS OF STATUS QUO
Positive thoughts & feelings about the current situation

CONS OF CHANGE
Fears about future

CHOICES AVAILABLE
Options & consequences for changing or not changing

CONS OF STATUS QUO
Negative thoughts & feelings about the current situation

PROS OF CHANGE
Hopes for future

POSSIBLE RESOLUTIONS *Given what you've learned, how might you move forward together?*

RESISTANCE

READINESS

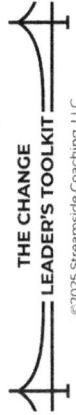

THE CHANGE LEADER'S TOOLKIT
©2025 Streamside Coaching, LLC

Figure 5 The Golden Bridge worksheet

- What are your top priorities?
- What is changing for your team/department?
- What is changing for you specifically?

Pros of status quo

Here, you will note any positive thoughts or feelings the person shares about the current situation. You might ask the following questions to surface this information:

- What do you think is going well?
- What do you like about how things are now?
- What would you like to stay the same?

Cons of change

Record any fears about the future the person shares with you. Try these questions:

- What would be different for you because of this change?
- How would you personally be affected by this change?
- What objections do you think other people might have?

» MIDDLE ROW MOVING TO READINESS

The second row focuses on co-creating options to increase readiness for change. As you talk through these prompts, you will use the inquiry and reflection techniques described above to amplify the change talk you hear.

Choices available

Note what options the other person believes they have available and the likely consequences of each choice. Questions you can ask to elicit options and likely consequences include the following:

- What options do you have?
- What will likely happen as a result of choosing that option?
- What will likely not occur as a result of selecting that option?
- What would you like to do?
- What would you most like to happen?

Cons of status quo

In this section, record the negative thoughts and feelings the person expresses about the current situation or status quo. To uncover these, ask questions like these:

- What challenges exist right now?
- What could be better about the current situation?
- What would you most like to improve?

Pros of change

Here, you will capture the person's hopes for the future with the change. Invite them to imagine possibilities by asking the following questions:

- What new possibilities might arise?
- What could happen if you were successful in making this change?
- How might things look a year from now?

» BOTTOM ROW POSSIBLE RESOLUTIONS

In the bottom row, write down any ideas or possibilities for productive paths you identified through the conversation. You can engage the other person in brainstorming possibilities with the following questions:

- What might be missing from this plan?
- What would have to be true for this change to benefit you?
- What would you suggest to make the change easier or better?
- What is the most important thing to get right about this change?
- What is the most important thing not to get wrong?
- What might improve outcomes for everyone?

UNEXPECTED DISCOVERIES ON THE OTHER SIDE

I have taught the Golden Bridge Framework to dozens of people in my workshops and hundreds more through live webinars. Occasionally, I have the privilege of hearing from one of the participants after they have applied these techniques to their real-world challenges.

Rebecca, who participated in one of my first workshops on this topic, shared a heartfelt story with me a few months after she learned about the golden bridge. Her elderly father had been struggling on his own, and Rebecca was making arrangements for him to move into her home so she could better manage his care. This was a difficult transition for both of them, and tempers often flared over seemingly trivial issues. One hot point was Rebecca's father's beloved recliner: it was badly worn and needed to be replaced, but he could not bear to part with it.

When Rebecca convinced her father to shop for a new chair, she used the golden bridge technique during the shopping trip to stay curious about what mattered to her father and explore options for moving forward. In the past, Rebecca might have pushed him to make a decision quickly, which would have immediately backfired. This time, she asked him what he liked about his old chair and helped him look for new options with features he would enjoy and that they both could live with. Rebecca told me proudly that there were several moments when she successfully shifted her thinking from frustration and irritation to empathy and openness. After navigating this experience successfully, Rebecca felt confident she could handle the other aspects of the change with more grace and patience than she thought she could.

What I loved most about this story was how Rebecca realized *she* had changed after approaching her father's resistance differently. The lovely outcome on the other side of the golden bridge was not only a solution to a problem—it was an entirely different perspective.

LISTENING TO WHAT REMAINS UNSAID

By seizing golden opportunities and building a golden bridge in your conversations about resistance, you have increased your opportunities to empathize with those affected by your change effort and understand the challenges they are experiencing.

Not all resistance is vocal, however. In many cases, resistance is expressed passively through silence or inaction.

What can we do in these cases? The temptation for many change leaders in the face of silence is to double down on sharing their message—to speak louder, longer, or more forcefully. This can be helpful, but often I find it distracts from what is needed more: listening intently to what remains unsaid.

I am especially attuned to what remains unsaid because of my longstanding fascination with the writer Ernest Hemingway. Hemingway was famous for his spare prose, and he described his work with reference to his theory of omission, also known as the iceberg theory. In Hemingway's writing, the deeper meaning is never explicitly mentioned and remains out of view. However, it can still be felt and understood, just as only the top of an iceberg is visible above the water, with the bulk remaining submerged beneath the surface.

This is just as true in everyday conversation as it is in literature. Most of what people are really thinking and feeling is beneath the surface. We have to listen deeply to sense what is going on.

For this reason, when facilitating a team meeting or event where change is at stake, I pay equal attention to what is *not* said to what is said. You can learn a great deal by noticing what and who is omitted from the conversation. A lack of criticism or silence is often a clue that something remains hidden. Other indicators are mismatches between word choice, vocal tone, energy or pacing, and body language. Although it is tempting to devise explanations and stories for what is happening, if you have taken the time to establish genuine rapport with someone, they will often tell you what is beneath the surface.

IN SUMMARY

Resistance is a perennial source of frustration for many change agents. In this chapter, we have explored some alternative ways of viewing resistance, including resistance as traction and the necessary role it plays in the change process.

Responding forcefully to resistance usually produces the opposite of the intended effect. Instead of pushing harder when we encounter resistance, we can choose a more productive path. Look for the vital information the person is sharing with you. Use this information to improve your approach and gain a new ally. Find a way to build a golden bridge you both can traverse to the other side.

You may be surprised by what you discover in the process.

5

Creating Shared Context

When I started coaching Laura, she was a senior manager with extensive operational expertise at a large Fortune 100 company. For the past eighteen months, Laura had been working toward a promotion to director. Her leaders gave her great feedback on her work, but the promotion remained out of reach. When Laura approached me about coaching, she was keen to accelerate her progress and land the role.

One of the areas we focused on in coaching was Laura's relationships with her peers. Laura had one colleague in particular who drove her crazy. Anna was a highly analytical technical leader and frequently opposed Laura directly when she shared her ideas for improving things. They had been locked in a stalemate for months when Laura and I started working together.

In one coaching session, Laura wondered aloud what she could do to make Anna see her point of view on an organizational redesign. I asked if she would be open to trying something different and walked her through the Action/Reaction Sequence described in Chapter One. After walking through the sequence together, Laura realized her colleague must be feeling some of the same pressures: she probably also wanted to prove herself and demonstrate that she was an expert in her domain.

In subsequent calls, we worked on a more subtle, patient approach for Laura to build the case for her initiatives with peers. Instead of pitching her ideas in a large forum (and inevitably battling her difficult colleague point for point on the merits of her vision), she started working behind the scenes. Laura would meet with others one-on-one or in small groups and share drafts of her proposals. She would invite feedback and adjust her plans based on what she heard. When it came time to deliver the pitch to Laura's leaders, she had a much more solid proposal that already had her peers' backing.

A few months later, Laura got the promotion she wanted. When she shared the good news with me, Laura credited our work together to develop her peer influence skills as a key part of her success.

Retrospectively, it was easy to see why this work had been crucial for Laura in achieving the promotion to the next level. For many leaders, especially in large organizations, the real gap in reaching the senior leadership ranks is not about technical ability—it is using influence to get things done. As Laura practiced and honed these skills throughout our coaching engagement, she demonstrated she could effectively balance multiple perspectives and make decisions for the greater organizational good without burning bridges.

This chapter will cover several strategies for laying the groundwork for collaborative change, just as Laura did. These include building consensus with the Japanese business philosophy of *nemawashi*, crafting a compelling case for change in collaboration with your sponsor and stakeholders, and mapping the political landscape. These strategies build on the self-management and relationship-building skills we explored in the preceding chapters. The work you do here will prepare you to secure necessary resources and leadership support for your change effort by forming a collaborative change leadership team, which is the focus of Chapter Six.

BUILDING CONSENSUS THROUGH NEMAWASHI

One of the techniques we used to enhance Laura's relationships with her peers is *nemawashi,* which I first learned about when I worked at Nissan. *Nemawashi* is a Japanese term that means "going around the roots." In a literal sense, it refers to preparing trees for transplantation. In Japanese business culture, it is a philosophy for gently and effectively promoting change.

If you have ever transplanted a tree or shrub, you can see how apt the metaphor is. If you try to simply uproot the plant, it will stubbornly stay put. If you dig too forcefully, you may damage the roots, and it will die. If you do not dig in a broad enough circle around the roots, you might get the plant mostly free, with one stubborn root holding the plant in place.

However, if you go gently around the tree and coax each root on its terms, the tree will release easily and thrive in its new home. This is precisely how skilled change agents make change look easy. The work is done quietly behind the scenes.

As a decision-making process, *nemawashi* almost always takes longer than convening everyone in a single meeting, debating in the open, and making a decision on the spot. When done correctly, *nemawashi* often results in smoother and swifter execution of the decision once it is made. In Japanese business culture, this trade-off is preferred: decide slowly and execute quickly.

If you have worked on a change initiative waylaid by resistance or blocked by unhappy stakeholders, you know how a seemingly simple change can slow to a crawl or be stopped entirely by inadequate or incomplete buy-in. Unfortunately, in our haste to get things done, we often rush past these steps and secure only surface-level support for our efforts. When things get difficult, we realize we have not dug deeply or far enough around the roots.

SHARED OWNERSHIP INSTEAD OF BUY-IN

To ensure your *nemawashi* practice is effective, approach your conversations with the intent of building shared ownership rather than merely securing buy-in for your ideas. This difference is subtle but essential. If you lack positional authority in an organization, you will need both meaningful sponsorship from a sufficiently powerful leader and effective teamwork with your peers for your change effort to be successful. Shared ownership means that your sponsor and your peers are significantly and personally invested in the success of the change.

How can you tell if others are significantly and personally invested? A straightforward way to test this is to consider what would happen to the change effort if you were to take a sudden leave of absence—would it continue to progress without your direct involvement? If you have approached others intending to build a participative and collaborative culture, the change effort is far more likely to persist even in your absence.

Is this not the same as gaining buy-in? In my view, no. Most people approach gaining buy-in with the enthusiasm and curiosity they lend to getting signatures on a petition. They are passionate about the cause but care much less about your interest in it. Once they get your signature, they are off knocking on the next door. Conversations geared toward gaining buy-in in this way are often superficial and structured toward closing the deal: yes or no.

By contrast, if you approach these conversations with the goal of shared ownership, you will not be content with a simple yes or no. Instead, you will be interested in learning what is at stake for each person if they support or oppose the change. You will want to discover what they could gain, what they could lose, and what leverage they have to influence the outcome. You will also want to hear their ideas. What would make the change effort more valuable for the organization? What issues will need to be overcome?

CREATING ALIGNMENT WITH THE NORTH STAR CANVAS

As you learn more about your peers' and sponsors' perspectives on the change, you may find it helpful to record your observations in a template I created called the Change Leader's North Star Canvas (Figure 6).

The Change Leader's North Star Canvas is a tool for iteratively refining your case for change based on what you learn from your various *nemawashi* conversations. Here are some guidelines for using it.

THE CHANGE LEADER'S NORTH STAR CANVAS

CHANGE INITIATIVE

DESIGNED BY

DATE

VERSION

CHANGE STATEMENT
We need to go from...

to...

VISION
What becomes possible when the change is successful

WHY THIS?
Benefits to the organization

WHY NOW?
How the timing matters

WHY ME?
How I'm qualified to lead

SIGNS OF SUCCESS
Leading & lagging indicators

RESOURCES
Time, money, political capital

KEY PARTNERS
Champions & stakeholders

HEADWINDS
Environmental factors making it harder to move forward

TAILWINDS
Environmental factors making it easier to move forward

THE CHANGE LEADER'S TOOLKIT
©2025 Streamside Coaching, LLC

FIGURE 6   The Change Leader's North Star Canvas

START WITH YOUR IDEAS

Start by filling out the canvas based on your ideas and assumptions about the change. Work from top to bottom, left to right, considering the prompts below.

» TOP ROW SETTING THE DIRECTION

Change statement
Begin with a simple, concise statement of the change. What are you moving from, and what are you moving toward?

Vision
What will be possible when the change is successful?

» MIDDLE ROW BUILDING MOMENTUM

Why this?
There could be many options for improving the current situation. Why do you believe the proposed change is the best path forward? What are the benefits?

Why now?
What is at stake? How does the timing matter? What would be the consequences of a delay? If the change had been considered previously and not acted on, what makes it essential to move ahead now?

Why me?
What makes you the best person to lead or facilitate this change? How do your perspective, skills, or position uniquely qualify you for the effort?

Signs of success
What are some early signs that the change is heading in the right direction? What outcome measures would confirm that the change has been successful?

Resources

What specific resources (e.g., time, money, equipment, personnel) do you need to be successful? What existing resources can you leverage? What might you need to request?

Key partners

Who else has an interest or stake in the change? Who will you need to partner with to implement the change successfully? Be sure to name the highest-level sponsor for this change. What are their goals and objectives? What are they willing to invest to ensure the change is successful?

» BOTTOM ROW CONSIDERING CONTEXT

Headwinds

What environmental factors make it more challenging to move ahead? Consider the current pressures and goals in the organization, as well as external factors. Are there other concurrent change initiatives competing for people's attention and focus?

Tailwinds

What environmental factors will make it easier to move forward? Consider internal strengths and external opportunities. What recent wins can you capitalize on to propel this new initiative?

After an initial pass, review what you have written. Are there areas you are unsure about? Note any open questions or assumptions you want to validate in conversations with your peers and sponsor.

MEET WITH THE SPONSOR

Next, meet with the highest-ranking person you believe will sponsor or champion the change. In this conversation, share your understanding of the change initiative and its importance to the organization. Ask the sponsor to share what makes this initiative important from their perspective. Do not shy away from asking direct questions about what they are willing to invest to support the change in terms of personal time, budget, and political capital. You will also want to touch on each element of the Change Leader's North Star Canvas to vet your understanding of the change effort and ensure you are aligned.

SPONSOR INTERVIEW QUESTIONS

Review the following questions to help you prepare for this conversation and decide which you would like to focus on in your meeting:

Why change?
- What makes this change necessary for the organization?
- How urgent is the change?
- What is at stake for the organization in making this change?
- What will likely happen if we do not make this change successfully?
- Relative to other initiatives currently in progress, how significant is this effort?

Leadership
- Do you believe I am the right person to lead or facilitate this effort?
- What do you see as my unique qualifications for leading or facilitating the change?

Vision
- What would success look like to you?
- What will be possible if we are successful with the change?

Sponsorship and resources
- What amount of time, energy, or money would you be willing to invest in helping this effort be successful?
- What level of involvement would you like to have in the change effort?
- Would you be willing to act as a sponsor or champion for this change?

Key partners
- How do you think others will receive the change in the organization?
- Who might be enthusiastic about the change?
- Who might have concerns?
- Who needs to be included in the working team?

Headwinds and tailwinds
- What factors might make it harder to move forward?
- What factors might make it easier to move forward?
- What issues need to be addressed along the way?

If the response is less than enthusiastic—or worse, you are unable to get a meeting with the sponsor—take note. You might be tempted to conclude that you can still move forward in a grassroots fashion and make progress regardless. Proceed with extreme caution! I have tested this tactic for years, and the results are almost always disappointing.

Instead of charging ahead with insufficient support, reflect on what you have learned from interacting with the sponsor. For change to be successful in the long term, the mainstream organizational culture must accept it. While everyone in an organization contributes to its culture, leaders are the most potent culture carriers: others take their cues from how the leaders act and what they choose to reward or punish. If your change effort is unimportant to the leaders you hope will champion it, you must contend with the real possibility that you are wasting your time.

Assuming your sponsor is interested in your change effort's success and has offered adequate support, return to your North Star Canvas and update it with a new version reflecting your learning. As you do this, you are strengthening and clarifying your case for change.

ARRANGE NEMAWASHI CONVERSATIONS

Continue the process by meeting with anyone you have noted in the "Key partners" section of the canvas. As you did with the sponsor, ask for their perspective on the ideas you have captured on the North Star Canvas. If they disagree with your views, do not engage in debate. Instead, practice the techniques we explored in Chapter Three for holding effective one-on-one conversations about change. Remember: this is not a sales pitch but a scouting mission. The more information you can gather about how people think about the change, the better positioned you will be to lead effectively.

Before you conclude your *nemawashi* conversations, ask each person if they can think of anyone with a stake in the change or another perspective to share. Continue to work in as wide a circle as possible. Update your North Star Canvas after each conversation to keep track of what you learn.

MAPPING THE POLITICAL LANDSCAPE

You should have had several conversations with many people about the change by now. As a result, you should have a much clearer and more well-rounded view of the change effort than when you started. Not all of this view will be rosy. You will have discovered that opinions about the change vary through your conversations. Any change—even widely popular ones—will have some detractors. That is okay. This is valuable information to have as you plan how to move forward.

The next step in the process is to take what you have learned about the change effort and the people involved to map the political landscape you are operating in. If you are anything like me, you might have been tempted to slam the book shut as you read that last sentence. Many of us, myself included, have developed a real disdain for organizational politics: it can feel slimy, underhanded, and manipulative. However, the truth I have begrudgingly come to accept is that politics is how things get done in organizations.

Through time and painful experience, I have learned that ignoring organizational politics is like ignoring gravity. Your willingness to acknowledge it is irrelevant. It is always there. Gravity is invisible but has power over everything in its force field. Organizational politics operate the same way. You do not have to like or accept this fact—they will act on you regardless.

To illustrate, I recently worked with a new executive charged with leading several transformational change initiatives. After a few months on the job, he realized his task was more complex than initially thought. While he had a clear vision of where he needed the organization to go, the real difficulty was aligning his peers' competing viewpoints. Several of them had long tenures with the company—although they lacked industry-leading expertise, they were nonetheless adept in the workings and politics of the firm. Without their partnership, my client's change initiatives would go nowhere. Understanding the political landscape and operating accordingly would be essential if he wanted to succeed.

This can be disappointing for those who have hoped a promotion to a new level of formal authority would make it easier to get folks to go along with their ideas. Ironically, the opposite is often true. As an individual contributor, you may only need to influence your boss to get agreement to move forward with an idea. If you are a team leader, you will now have to consider how to pitch your ideas in at least three dimensions: to your boss, your direct reports, and your peers. This is why the *nemawashi* process is so crucial. If you understand what people have to gain, what they have to lose, and what leverage they have over your effort, you can be proactive in your communication and expectation management.

THE INFLUENCE-INVESTMENT LENS

A simple way to map the political landscape is to consider two key dimensions: the extent of a stakeholder's influence within the organization and their level of investment in the outcome. To visualize this, use a two-by-two grid with influence on the vertical axis and investment on the horizontal axis (see Figure 7).

Let's start with the left half of the grid. Stakeholders with low influence and low investment map to the bottom left quadrant, labeled "check in." Because they are not significantly invested in the effort and have little ability to influence it, you need not spend much time managing expectations for people in this group. A semi-regular check-in should suffice. Stakeholders with high influence and low investment map to the top right box, labeled "communicate." You will want to invest more effort in your change communications with this group. While these individuals

THE INFLUENCE-INVESTMENT GRID

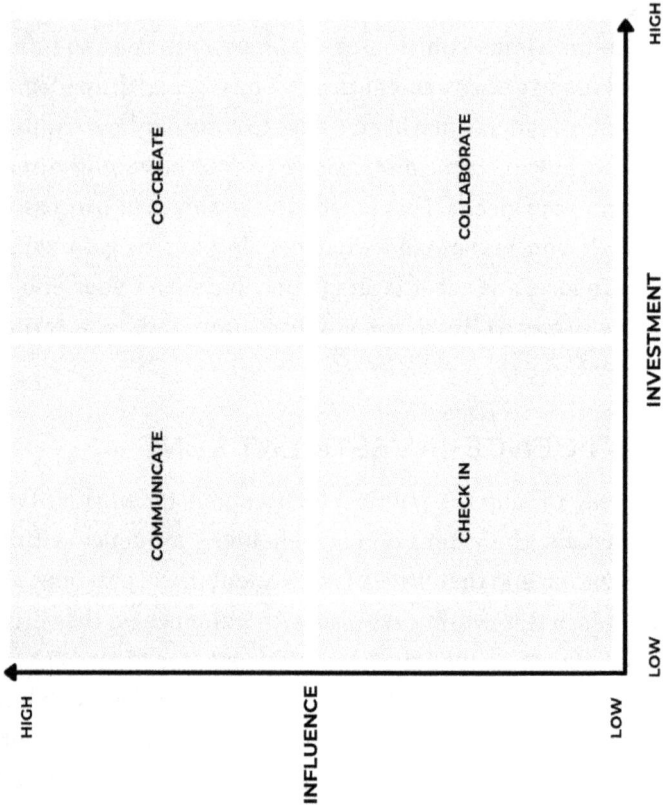

Figure 7 The Influence-Investment Grid

may not have a significant personal stake in the change effort, their high level of influence in the organization makes it important to keep them informed throughout the process.

On the right half of the grid are the quadrants labeled "collaborate" and "co-create." Stakeholders with high investment and low influence map to the "collaborate" quadrant, and stakeholders with both high investment and high influence map to the "co-create" quadrant. These two groups will have the most significant influence on the success of your effort. Stakeholders in the "collaborate" quadrant are most likely to be personally affected by the change in their day-to-day operations. These individuals can provide detailed information about the ground-level change experience and offer helpful suggestions for improvements. Stakeholders in the "co-create" quadrant are also highly invested in the change while possessing the organizational influence to steer the strategic direction. These individuals make excellent candidates for your change leadership team, which will be discussed in greater detail in Chapter Six.

When I shared this tool with a client, she had a few important realizations. My client was a member of a senior leadership team at a startup that had recently been acquired by a larger firm. She knew she needed to spend more time building relationships with her peers at the new firm, but was unsure where to start. Her role was already quite demanding, so we used the Influence-Investment Grid to help her prioritize her relationship-building efforts. After mapping the company's leaders and stakeholders on the grid, my client realized she had been treating her most powerful stakeholder—one of the executives at the acquiring firm—far too casually. This person was heavily invested in my client's work and had the power and influence to have the board remove her as an officer of the company if he saw fit. Following this insight, my client devoted much more thought to preparing for their monthly meetings.

After mapping stakeholders to the Influence-Investment Grid, look closer at the names you have listed in the top row. What might each person stand to gain or lose from this effort? Make sure you understand the specific gains and losses at stake for each person and the leverage they have to influence the direction of your effort. Your *nemawashi* conversations will be an excellent source of this information.

BRING THEM LAURELS

When I was a project manager, one of my mentors would remind me to "always bring them laurels," recalling the ancient Roman tradition of crowning the commanders of military victories with laurel wreaths. What he meant by this was that an essential part of our job was ensuring our sponsors and most powerful stakeholders realized gains from our efforts. Depending on your viewpoint about organizational politics, you might find this notion ridiculous or repellant, but I would encourage you to consider the pragmatic good sense it conveys.

Change introduces uncertainty, and navigating through uncertainty requires risk-taking. Our task as change facilitators is to make it possible for people to move forward, even when a great deal may be at stake. We cannot always minimize the risks of a negative outcome, but we can do our best to reduce the reputational risks sponsors and peers take when they bet on an uncertain path. You can move things forward by finding options for everyone to benefit from the effort.

IN SUMMARY

In this chapter, we covered several strategies for establishing a shared context for your change effort. Each strategy—building consensus through *nemawashi*, creating alignment with the North Star Canvas, and mapping the political landscape—deepens our shared understanding of what might be required for the change to be successful.

For many change agents, especially those who like to move quickly, taking the time to establish a shared context can feel unbearably slow. It can also be disheartening—we may discover conflicting viewpoints and challenging environmental factors that make the change effort appear hopelessly complex.

Don't despair. If you use these techniques on your own initiative, you will gain valuable insights while simultaneously building the relationships you need to move forward. It pays to be patient and methodical.

6

Securing Leadership Support

Several years ago, I was a product manager at a small health-care consulting company, leading the development of an internal software application. The purpose of the software was to improve internal operations by streamlining and centralizing key reporting processes. Until then, the administrative staff collected data in Excel sheets and manually refined it into printed reports for distribution at weekly staff meetings. They spent many hours each week painstakingly compiling, formatting, printing, and collating the thick reports, which were used once and thrown away.

The company leaders saw an opportunity to optimize this process and knew the data contained other valuable insights hidden from view. So they hired a small team of contractors (two developers and me, the product manager) to transform their weekly Excel-based reports into a mobile-responsive Web application. Our user base included roughly sixty senior employees—regional vice presidents, associate vice presidents, and financial analysts. In their consulting roles at the company, they guided top administrators at troubled rural hospitals. Most had been hospital CEOs or CFOs before joining the firm, with at least thirty years of experience in their field.

My previous roles had been at younger tech companies, where the employees tended to be digital natives and up-to-date on the latest technology. At this company, I learned through one-on-one interviews with several users that many had never learned how to type on a computer. "I didn't take typing in high school forty years ago," one regional vice president told me. "And honestly, I haven't needed it. My admin prints my emails for me, and she types up what I handwrite or dictate."

From these early conversations, I realized that launching a successful software product would require much more than developing solid technology and assuming our users would figure out how to use it. We had to deeply understand our users and their current processes to design a product they would adopt. We also had to help them become accustomed to a new way of working while ensuring they could continue doing their jobs without interruption.

We succeeded. Within a few months, we had transitioned the most critical reports to the new software application, saving many hours of manual labor each week. Our users, who had been skeptical initially, became highly invested in the project, providing regular feedback on new features and offering suggestions for improving the application. When it came time to pitch the CEO for a capital investment to continue development and expand the application a year later, he responded, "How much do you want?" He agreed on the spot to our full request of $1.3 million.

This was possible because a highly effective change leadership team was working behind the scenes. The members included the leaders of each user role (three senior vice presidents), the CIO, the CFO, and me as the product manager. This team performed several essential functions:

- Aligned development efforts with the company's strategic objectives.
- Regularly communicated the importance of the initiative with users and stakeholders.
- Ensured the needs of the users and all other stakeholders were appropriately identified, balanced, and prioritized.
- Secured the material and political resources the development team needed to create valuable software, including direct user access for ongoing feedback.
- Co-created user acceptance testing and pilot testing plans to ensure business continuity while users learned how to use the software.
- Met regularly to discuss the project's progress and direction.
- Addressed user concerns and complaints about the technology and the business process changes in a constructive manner.

I was by far the least influential person on the team. My role was levels below the other members in the organizational hierarchy, and I was decades younger and a contractor. Regardless, the change leadership team members treated me as a trusted and valued partner, and I strove to show up as one.

I share this story to make two points. First, successful organizational change is almost always led by a team, not an individual. You need a team to ensure your effort receives the necessary support and resources to get things done. Second, you do not need to be "in charge" or even at a peer level in the organizational hierarchy to build an effective change leadership team. You can do this, no matter what your role is.

If you are skeptical about the first point, consider the second step in John Kotter's well-known eight-step change framework: "Creating the guiding coalition" (2012).[2] As Kotter asserts, teams are needed to lead change successfully (2012). Without the support of an aligned team, even most CEOs cannot accomplish their transformational change goals. For those of us who are positioned in the middle of the organization and lack formal authority, it should be no surprise that we, too, will need a robust team collaborating with us to get things done.

If you are unsure about the second point—that you can build an effective change leadership team regardless of your title or role—I want to assure you that it is possible. No magic is required; you simply have to design and launch the team thoughtfully. The following pages will explore why and how to do this.

WHY YOU NEED A LEADERSHIP TEAM FOR YOUR CHANGE EFFORT

When I introduce this concept in my training programs, people commonly ask how a change leadership team differs from the working team executing the project. "We have a sponsor for the initiative," they say. "Isn't that enough?"

Typically, no. Most organizational change efforts span multiple boundaries, involving diverse teams and stakeholders with varying interests. Your boss likely explained the importance of the change when assigning you to the effort, but others involved may not have received similar instructions from their leaders.

---

2   From *Harvard Business Review*, "Leading Change: Why Transformation Efforts Fail" by John P. Kotter. Published January 2007. Copyright © 2007 Harvard Business School Publishing Corporation. Excerpt reprinted with permission of the publisher.

For you, the change effort's success is a high priority; this may not be the case for others. To address this imbalance, you may feel pressure to make the change a priority for others despite the implicit message from their leaders that the change is not.

Rather than resorting to coercion and force as we often do in such situations, we can leverage the power dynamics inherent in the organizational hierarchy to do the heavy lifting for us. The most straightforward and ethical way to do this is to convene a change leadership team representing the highest levels of leadership who have a direct interest in the change effort.

If this sounds daunting, first consider the benefits. When you have all the necessary stakeholders in the room, you can align your effort with strategic priorities, secure resources, and develop clear plans for integrating the change into existing work habits. You will have access to existing communication channels for everyone affected by the change. With leadership support, the change will have credibility and political weight. You will be far more likely to succeed and won't have to do it alone.

ALIGNING EFFORTS

Something almost magical happens when you convene all the relevant stakeholders for your change effort in one room and invite them to lead together as a team. You bring everything into the light. Assumptions come sharply into view, making it instantly clear why things are or aren't working.

Change efforts fail because we lack alignment and shared understanding. This lack of alignment often results from well-meaning assumptions we have neglected to validate with the others involved. We might, for example, assume that everyone shares the same priorities or that we all stand to benefit from the change. We might assume we have explained the need for the change clearly and that others see the context similarly. We may believe we have provided adequate resources and time to ensure the change will be successful. We would likely persist in these assumptions until someone else confronts us with a different perspective.

Convening a change leadership team creates a forum for these conversations to happen naturally. If you proactively form the team before the initiative is underway, you can create alignment on the core issues before misunderstandings become problematic. You will also have a forum for addressing new issues as they arise. Moreover, by centering these conversations in a team setting, you set the expectation that the group will arrive at their decisions jointly. You may need to facilitate to help the team reach a consensus, but conducting these conversations in the open is far easier than shuttling the negotiating positions of multiple aloof executives through diplomatic back channels.

In the example I shared, the change leadership team's monthly meetings offered a regular touchpoint for stakeholders to align on the project's strategic direction. Each month, we would review the current progress and discuss our upcoming plans. Sometimes, our work would benefit one stakeholder group far more than the others. We would debate the options and determine the direction together as a team. As the team's facilitator, this process simplified my work and relieved the burden of justifying the project's direction to unhappy stakeholders in one-on-one conversations.

SECURING RESOURCES

When you assemble a sufficiently empowered change leadership team, securing the resources you need to succeed will be far more straightforward. Make sure you ask for what you need. One benefit of building a change leadership team is that they can make things happen. Most of us who have spent our careers at the middle levels of organizations are adept at coping with limited resources. If you have worked to gain alignment and support, use it! Leaders who have agreed to join your change leadership team want your effort to succeed. Allow them to help by using their power and authority to make good things happen.

One resource that can be difficult to obtain without leadership support is direct access to the people affected by the change. Our software project greatly benefited from a dedicated user testing and feedback process we developed in collaboration with the change leadership team. We established a rotating schedule of two-week intervals for gathering user feedback. During their assigned interval, we would invite two individuals from the user group to test new features and provide feedback. This process helped us learn what was most valuable to our users while boosting their confidence in the software's usefulness. Without direct involvement from the change leadership team, gaining this level of regular engagement would have been much more challenging.

INTEGRATING THE CHANGE

Many change initiatives fail to account for existing work demands and competing priorities. While the change initiative may be a top priority for leaders, it won't become one for staff until it is made clear what needs to be deprioritized to accommodate the change. In the absence of clear guidance indicating otherwise, people maintain the status quo. What is often perceived as resistance is a reflection of this gap in communication.

Therefore, one key function of the change leadership team is to assess the change's impact on current workloads and existing projects and devise reasonable plans for integrating the change while accounting for these realities. For our software project, the change leadership team was instrumental in designing a thoughtful pilot testing and implementation plan that provided ample time for learning the new process while ensuring business continuity. For one reporting period, the leaders directed their teams to use the new software in parallel with their existing process. While this temporarily duplicated the team's efforts, it provided a low-risk opportunity to identify any issues with the new software. Once the user group was satisfied they could continue their work satisfactorily, the leaders announced that they would discontinue using the old process and rely exclusively on the new software.

ACCESSING THE TEAM'S COMMUNICATION NETWORKS

One of the benefits of convening a change leadership team is gaining access to the team members' existing communication networks to help you integrate the change into the current work environment. These existing networks allow you to share information and listen to people's opinions about the change with relatively little startup cost.

Leveraging the existing networks makes communication efforts much more straightforward and effective. As marketers will tell you, it is far easier to capitalize on someone else's audience than to build your own from scratch. Use what is already there to create opportunities for dialogue. You will need support from the leaders in charge of these channels to use these existing networks and established communication forums, so recruiting these individuals to your change leadership team is vital.

If you do not have this support, you must develop your own means of communication. Setting up a meeting or sending an email is easy, but getting people's attention in modern workplaces is considerably more difficult. Calendars are chronically overbooked and emails are skimmed if read at all. Often, the easiest way to get someone's attention is to have the message come from their boss, so take advantage of this if you can.

We capitalized on this advantage for the software project in several ways. As many change projects commonly do, we used a large kickoff meeting to explain the high-level goals and scope of the project. Instead of planning a separate event, the executives on the change leadership team invited me to speak at an upcoming quarterly meeting and introduce the effort to the staff. This event was an excellent opportunity to connect in person with our users, who spent most of their time on the road visiting client sites.

My primary goal for the kickoff presentation was to open a dialogue between the software's users and the development team. To accomplish this, I explained the feedback process we would use to develop the software and invited our users to our bi-weekly project meetings. I also wanted to establish early rapport with the user group, so I asked them to share feedback on the initiative's overall goals. I intended for everyone to leave the presentation understanding how they would benefit from participating in the project.

With this context established, gaining interest in our project meetings was much more manageable. Two weeks later, several users attended our first demo and feedback session. We began by sharing the work we had committed to deliver, noting what we finished and where we fell short. Then, the developers gave a live demonstration of the working software they created, and we asked for feedback from the audience.

We repeated this process every two weeks. If we learned that something did not meet expectations, we would thank the person for letting us know and schedule a time to follow up on the specifics later. At the subsequent demo, we shared how we had incorporated user feedback to make improvements.

In parallel with our regular project meetings, each of the senior vice presidents on the change leadership team regularly included me on the agenda for their monthly staff meetings. Each month, I would attend for the first ten minutes to share an update on the software project's progress and ask for any feedback from the group. By visiting each group on their "home turf," we dramatically increased the likelihood that more people would hear the message and share their views in response.

Interleaving these two communication strategies ensured we could regularly reach most of our user base to share updates and important messages. It also helped position the development team as highly accessible and open to user input and feedback. As a result, we had high user adoption and minimal resistance to the overall effort.

FORMING YOUR CHANGE LEADERSHIP TEAM

As you form a change leadership team for your own change initiative, you may find it helpful to record your notes on the Change Leadership Team Design worksheet (Figure 8). Include your initial thoughts about the team's purpose, key tasks, composition, potential candidates, rhythms, and context. We will explore these elements each in turn.

ARTICULATING THE TEAM'S PURPOSE

The first question to consider as you form your change leadership team is the team's purpose. The purpose should resonate at the level of the entire team and the level of each member. A clearly articulated team purpose will help you to establish a sense of shared ownership and interdependence among the change leadership team members. For the team to work together effectively, they will need to see themselves as a cohesive unit, rather than a collection of individual leaders jockeying for influence over the initiative. All team members should be invested in the outcome and want to help the team achieve its goals.

You will continue to refine the purpose in the early stages of assembling your team, but you should have a solid first draft derived from your work on the North Star Canvas. Revisit the

CHANGE LEADERSHIP TEAM DESIGN WORKSHEET

TEAM NAME **DURATION** **LAUNCH DATE**

CHANGE INITIATIVE

TEAM PURPOSE *What outcomes must the team deliver?*

KEY TEAM TASKS *What are primary duties of the team?*

TEAM COMPOSITION *What skills and perspectives are needed on the team?*

	TEAM ROLE / FUNCTION	DECISION-MAKING AUTHORITY
1		
2		
3		
4		
5		
6		
7		
8		
9		

CANDIDATES *Who are the right people to include?*

	NAME	ROLE	INFLUENCE-INVESTMENT
1			
2			
3			
4			
5			
6			
7			
8			
9			

TEAM RHYTHMS *When and how often will we meet and communicate as a team?*

TEAM CONTEXT *What will make the team's work easier or harder?*

THE CHANGE
LEADER'S TOOLKIT

Figure 8 The Change Leadership Team Design worksheet

following sections: Change statement, Vision, Why this?, and Why now? What picture emerges about what this team must do? How would you summarize this succinctly? You will need to convey this purpose concisely to recruit leaders to the team.

For the software project in this chapter, the primary purpose of the change leadership team was to ensure that the development efforts supported the business goals and objectives, so we referred to the team as the "Steering Committee." This language suited the company's formal culture and gave a clear sense of purpose for convening the group. The team also assumed secondary responsibilities for communications and facilitating user adoption to support their primary objective of stewarding the company's investment in the project.

IDENTIFYING KEY TASKS

What key tasks and functions will the team need to perform to accomplish its purpose? The work of the change leadership team will be distinct from that of a working team charged with implementing the change. The leadership team's tasks will focus on activities that only the leaders have the authority to perform; for example, setting strategic direction, apportioning resources, authorizing process and procedural changes, and facilitating communications with their staff.

In contrast with a working team's typical tasks, the change leadership team's primary responsibility is decision-making. What decisions may need to be made along the way? What approvals will be required? Brainstorming the possibilities will help you determine the expertise, authority, and political capital needed to ensure the team can deliver on its purpose.

DETERMINING TEAM COMPOSITION

Before determining who will be on the team, consider what roles and functions are necessary for the change effort to succeed. What influence or authority will the team require to secure resources and make decisions? Which roles are best suited for the unique tasks only the change leadership team can perform?

For the software development project, the change leadership team's key tasks were to set the strategic priorities for the product roadmap, manage communications with the user base, and make business process decisions that would affect their departments. As the technology product manager, I could not have accomplished these tasks alone because I lacked the formal authority and political capital. Each task required the support and shared direction of the change leadership team.

As you determine the composition of your change leadership team, make sure you consider the team size. You want to keep the team small (fewer than ten members) to facilitate effective communication and decision-making. The smaller the team, the less likely it is that there will be awkwardly overlapping responsibilities or the social loafing that plagues larger teams.

In some organizations, there is social pressure to include more people than necessary on a team to avoid the perception that certain individuals have been "left out" of discussions they feel they have a stake in. I tend to be unsympathetic to these kinds of arguments. There should be a clear purpose for each person's inclusion on the team. You are making a costly trade if you include an unnecessary individual to bypass an uncomfortable conversation. In exchange for avoiding momentary unpleasantness, you will have to endure a *series* of awkward conversations (e.g., *"Why is so-and-so on the team?"*) throughout their involvement. Extraneous people add unhelpful friction and slow decision-making. Less is almost always more.

Generally, there should not be more than one person per key function or role on the team. The only exception to this rule would be including your boss. If your boss believes they do not need to be on the change leadership team, make sure you are proactive about keeping them updated on the latest developments, regardless.

IDENTIFYING CANDIDATES

As you worked through the *nemawashi* process described in Chapter Five, you learned who has a stake in your change effort and who the most influential and powerful players are. These are the people you want on your team. Take a look at the Influence-Investment Grid you created. The individuals listed on the top right quadrant of the map are your first candidates for the change leadership team. How do these individuals fulfill the role and function needs you identified on the Change Leadership Team Design worksheet? Are there any gaps or overlaps? Write down who you plan to invite to the team next to the role and the function each will serve.

Next, review the notes from your stakeholder conversations. What did each of these people say they were willing to invest in helping the effort succeed? How much time, energy, money, or political capital have they offered to spend? If they have already committed to investing their time, this is your cue to invite them to join the change leadership team.

What should you do if some people you need on the team aren't particularly interested in participating? Take this as an indicator that you may need to articulate the team's purpose more clearly. You may also invest more time in understanding the specific pressures, goals, and motivations under which this individual operates.

If a stakeholder declines your invitation to join the team, play the diplomat. First, share why you asked for their participation.

Second, inquire about their perspective and whether they have any alternative suggestions, such as naming a delegate or participating on a more limited basis. Third, ask what would need to be different for participating to be worth their time. This question can reveal a simple solution. For example, adjusting the meeting timing or frequency may be all that is needed for the person to participate.

Sometimes, you must move forward with less than a complete team. Perhaps a key leader is too busy to participate regularly and delegates to a staff member, or someone whose support you desperately need is opposed to the effort and refuses to participate. In these situations, my strategy is to move forward with those enthusiastic about participating while leaving the door open to welcome those who might choose to join us later. What I mean by this is carefully and thoughtfully including these individuals in communications, asking for their opinions at reasonable intervals, and thanking them sincerely for any involvement they offer. Just because someone does not initially see the value in a change does not mean they will continue to hold that perspective. Give them plenty of room to change their minds.

ESTABLISHING TEAM RHYTHMS

Before convening the team, consider how long it will need to work together to accomplish its aims and what kind of time commitment the members will need to make. Make sure your requests are appropriate for the significance of the change effort. Most leadership teams do not require full-time participation to deliver on their goals; in many cases, an hour or two per month of shared meeting time may be sufficient. However, individuals with competing commitments and priorities may struggle to meet regularly and make real progress as a team.

The change leadership team for my software project first

convened at the beginning of the project and continued to meet regularly throughout the development process. Each person on the team was invested in the project's success and viewed their contribution to the team as essential to delivering on the strategic objectives of the initiative. Because all the change leadership team members were committed to the project, we had no problems securing the time, attention, and collaboration required to get things done.

Once you have determined how long the team will need to collaborate, the next step is to define a cadence for regular meetings and other communications. How frequently will you meet? What topics will be covered? Who will facilitate?

Our change leadership team met for one to two hours every two weeks to review progress and align priorities throughout the project. We also collaborated in different ways (e.g., one-on-one calls, attending each other's staff meetings, and *ad hoc* conversations) between the formal team meetings. This structure worked well to keep the change leadership team in sync without requiring excessive time. A different arrangement may work better for your effort.

Consider including a regular *team retrospective* in your meeting cadence. The idea is to reflect on the team's performance at frequent intervals and discuss what you might want to change or experiment with to improve your effectiveness as a team. Setting these conversations on the calendar in advance relieves much of the unspoken tension that can surface. Because all members know there will be an opportunity to discuss issues and find constructive paths forward, there are not as many unpleasant surprises or unexpected blow-ups. This meeting normalizes conversations about team dynamics and ensures the team addresses issues before they become intolerable.

You can also accomplish the same purpose with a lightweight set of questions at the end of your regular team meetings. You might refer to this as a "brief team check-in" and ask each person to share their thoughts about what is working particularly well and what might be helpful to improve or do differently.

ASSESSING THE TEAM'S CONTEXT

Assessing the team's context involves considering how it will access needed resources and address obstacles to progress. The Headwinds and Tailwinds sections of the North Star Canvas will offer clues about the organizational context, including potential challenges and opportunities. What opportunities could you capitalize on? What challenges exist in the current environment? The closer you can align your team's effort with the organization's broader strategic goals, the easier it will be to gain momentum.

Based on what you have learned about the organizational and environmental headwinds and tailwinds, what might make the change leadership team's work more difficult? For example, many competing initiatives could be underway that could limit access to resources. Perhaps there is tension or competition between members of the change leadership team. How might you address these challenges as a team when they arise?

Consider also what might make the team's work easier. How could you capitalize on momentum from related initiatives, recent successes, or strategic priorities? Look for synergies and alliances that you can build on to amplify your efforts.

For our software project, an organizational headwind (declining sales) served as a critical tailwind for our efforts. The company needed to gain internal efficiencies to offset revenue losses. It also needed to identify new opportunities to capitalize on existing data and assets for potential income streams. Our project would help with both of these things. Because the change leadership team understood the initiative's strategic importance for the broader organization, they treated their work on the team as a priority.

LAUNCHING THE TEAM

As with any other kind of team, a change leadership team needs a successful launch to set the foundation for the team's work together. The launch should orient the team to their shared tasks and each other.

Keep it simple and stay focused on the essentials. You will not be able to define and discuss everything needed throughout your work together during your launch event. You should, however, aim to leave the team launch with a solid foundation for the next step in your collaboration. Here are the minimum outcomes you should strive to accomplish in your team launch:

Introductions

Each person should know who everyone on the team is, their roles, what they hope to gain from participating, and how to pronounce their names correctly.

Shared purpose

The team should have a defined purpose all members fully support.

Vision and strategic direction

All members should understand and support the vision and the strategic direction, including the team's immediate priorities for their work.

Team conduct norms

The team should have a written list of conduct agreements all members support and agree to uphold, including the team's decision-making and conflict-resolution processes.

Meeting and communication cadence

The team should agree on the initial frequency and duration of their regular meetings and other communications. Identify which communication channels team members prefer and which methods are off-limits.

IN SUMMARY

Leading change is not a solo effort. Nearly all successful organizational change initiatives are the work of teams. If you are leading change without positional authority, building an effective change leadership team will be crucial to your success.

How you structure the team will affect the ease of your collaboration. Consider who needs to be included and what communication structures and resources are required to deliver on the team's purpose. Organize an intentional team launch to create clarity, alignment, and momentum.

Sometimes, we rush past these steps because we are eager to get started. The result is almost always a short burst of activity followed by a long period of floundering. Choose to be deliberate and thoughtful at this stage. With a solid team design and thoughtful team launch, you will be well on your way to making excellent progress.

7

Personal Resilience

As you have likely gathered by now, I am passionate about developing change leadership skills because of the opportunity it creates for personal growth—not just at work but in other facets of our lives. We grow through a process that naturally benefits others. This chapter will explore how leading and experiencing difficult change can facilitate our growth as change leaders—specifically, examining our thinking, extending our empathy, and learning to let go.

EXAMINING OUR THINKING

Many people will tell you that the most challenging aspect of change is dealing with the uncertainty it brings. In the face of the unknown, our usual assumptions become invalid. We are unsure how to act or what to think. We lose our direction and feel stuck. I recently worked with a coaching client who experienced this when his department was thrust into uncertainty after a senior leader left. Would his team be restructured? When would a new leader be named? How would this affect the team's goals and direction? My client wondered: did continuing down the current path make sense when it could all be swept away?

I have also found myself stuck in similarly spiraling thoughts during times of uncertainty and change. Over the years, I have become more curious and introspective about my patterns of reaction to unwanted change or unwelcome resistance. I tend to succumb to all manner of distorted thought patterns, particularly ones like the following:

- Viewing things in black-and-white or all-or-nothing terms
- Assuming fault for things that are mostly or entirely out of my control
- Making wild, catastrophic predictions about the future
- Torturing myself with a never-ending litany of "shoulds"

I'm not unique in this way. Cognitive behavioral therapists have long cataloged these thought patterns, and helpful, evidence-based interventions for interrupting the automatic negative spiral they induce. But because these thoughts are so automatic, it can be difficult to recognize them as irrational and unhelpful as they occur. Noticing the thought and identifying it is the first step. The longer these irrational, automatic thoughts go unchecked, the more damage they do.

At one organization, I shared a classic, evidence-based technique for identifying and reframing unhelpful thought patterns with several groups of leaders contending with a painful series of deep budget cuts and layoffs. In the exercise, I asked the participants to consider a hypothetical scenario in which a leader learns that the budget for the product he manages has been eliminated. Then, I asked them to respond to the following prompts: If you were this leader, what would you be feeling? What might you be thinking?

The responses to the feelings prompt were overwhelmingly negative: frustrated, worried, anxious, depressed, angry, disappointed, fearful, panicky. Here are some examples of the responses to the thinking prompt:

- "Are we all going to be fired?"
- "What do I tell my team? They'll all look for new jobs."
- "The last year has been a total waste!"
- "This is all my fault."
- "I shouldn't be upset. It's just business."

We could quickly identify several distorted thought patterns when we looked at these hypothetical responses together. Review the list of common thought distortions below. Which ones do you notice?

COMMON UNPRODUCTIVE THOUGHT PATTERNS

Black-and-white thinking
Extreme either/or thinking with no middle ground

Emotional reasoning
Using feelings as evidence to support a belief instead of verifiable facts

Catastrophizing
Predicting a catastrophe without considering more likely outcomes

Mind-reading
Making assumptions about what others think

Fortune-telling
Predicting the future without facts or evidence

Personalization
Assuming blame for problems outside your control

Magnification
Exaggerating the impact of a negative event

Irrational shoulds
Focusing on internal rules regardless of the context

The next step in the exercise was to reframe the automatic, distorted thought with something more balanced, rational, and empathetic. Here are some examples:

- *"Are we all going to be fired?"* became *"All I know now is that the product budget has been eliminated. We will probably be assigned to work on something else."*
- *"What do I tell my team? They'll all look for new jobs."* became *"I don't know how my team will respond. I can be honest and supportive when I share the news."*
- *"The last year has been a total waste!"* became *"It's disappointing that the product was canceled, but we learned many valuable things to apply to our next project."*
- *"This is all my fault."* became *"There are many factors that go into these decisions."*
- *"I shouldn't be upset. It's just business."* became *"This work is important to me, so it's natural to be upset."*

As we completed the exercise, I asked the participants to put themselves again in the shoes of the hypothetical product leader and consider how he might be feeling after reframing his thoughts in this way. The responses were quite different from where we began:

- Calmer.
- More in control.
- Relieved.
- Ready to think about what comes next.

Then, I asked the participants to reflect on their feelings about the changes they were experiencing after doing this exercise for the hypothetical leader. They felt better, too. We tend to feel much better when we shift our thoughts into more balanced, rational territory.

From teaching this exercise and using it myself, I have learned that negative reactions to change are natural and automatic.

They are also not permanent or indicative of how we will feel after we have had time to process what has happened and explore options for our next steps. For me, this serves as a powerful empathy-builder and a reminder of how important it is to give people (myself included!) the room to come to terms with the change before asking them to move forward.

EXTENDING OUR EMPATHY

My best teachers about change have been people I have experienced as difficult, uncooperative, or hostile to my efforts. Each of them has shown me the faulty assumptions in my thinking, the arrogance in my beliefs, and the limits of my generosity and patience. Whenever these things have been forced into view, I have had to re-examine my behavior, thoughts, and feelings about change and consider how my perspective may be only partially correct.

One of the most transformative experiences I've had in this regard was an exchange with a leader while working as an Agile coach. I sat down at my desk one day and found the following message in my inbox:

"How dare you send an email like this without consulting me! You had absolutely no right to do this. With this thoughtless message, you've completely eroded the trust I've spent months building with my business partner. I demand a meeting with you and your manager at once!"

I was stunned. Where did this come from? I thought I was being helpful!

Earlier that day, a fellow Agile coach and I emailed the IT leader and business sponsor of a new Agile team we had just started coaching. This response was the opposite of what we expected. In our discovery conversations, the IT leader and business sponsor had told us how enthusiastic they were about Agile. They were friendly, upbeat, and open to our suggestions.

But, after a few early conversations with the team, we learned that our definition of Agile as coaches seemed quite different from the one the sponsors were so enthusiastic about. One of the senior team members shared a detailed project plan with us, including the dates when various contract staff would join and depart the team. There was a planning phase, an analysis phase, a development phase, and a testing phase. This would be a problem—nothing about the team design or the work plan aligned with Agile principles or methods.

In the spirit of transparency, we jointly emailed the manager and the business sponsor to explain the situation. We tried to be clear and direct: "The design for this team and project does not align with Agile methods. The following changes are required..."

We fully expected to receive a response that began with "thank you" and continued with a hearty embrace of our suggestions. Reflecting on this situation several years later, I am amused by my naivete. I did not consider even momentarily how my email could offend the leader I was trying to help.

While I would love to believe in a world where senior leaders are always considerate, magnanimous, and open to feedback, this is unrealistic. Like all people, senior leaders have reputations they need to maintain and interests to protect. This does not make them bad people or leaders—it makes them human! By "educating" this leader on the misalignment of his stated desire and his design in my email, I inadvertently portrayed him as ignorant and incompetent in front of a person he needed to impress. Naturally, he was livid!

This experience, along with several others like it, catalyzed my professional coaching journey. Driving home that night, I felt angry, hurt, and misunderstood. I fumed, thinking about the email exchange, convinced that leaders are always the problem and that their actions keep teams stuck in the status quo.

And then I started to wonder: What would it be like to truly empathize with *this* person? What would it be like if I could serve him *and* the team? How might I change if I saw my job as supporting *everyone* in the system instead of protecting the team from their bosses?

Thinking this way challenged me to examine my role in the dynamic that led to this exchange. I was not the unfortunate and undeserving victim of a leader's wrath, as I initially wanted to believe. I was complicit. My attitude toward this leader—and leaders more generally—undermined my purpose. When there was conflict, my default posture was to blame the leader for the team's struggles. I would reflexively step in to "save" the team, unwittingly setting up a zero-sum game with winners and losers. The result of these games was almost always a Pyrrhic victory. If the leader won, the team would be demoralized. If the team and I won, the leader would lose face and often feel the need to reassert their authority more forcefully in the next conflict. Either scenario reduced the team's overall effectiveness, which was precisely the outcome I sought to avoid.

When I work with leaders, teams, and organizations now, I focus on maintaining positive regard for everyone in the larger system. I remind myself of the professional coaching principle that my clients are naturally creative and resourceful. If I genuinely believe that everyone I work with is creative and resourceful, there is no need to rescue anyone. There is also no need to cast blame. As a coach, I am much more effective when I approach *everyone* with the desire to serve and let my empathy extend in all directions.

LEARNING TO LET GO

As I have shared several times in this book, one of the most challenging aspects of change for me is accepting that I am not in control. I have been working on this for the last two decades. Whenever I think I have mastered the mindset to adapt to uncertainty, something reminds me that this will be a lifelong learning journey, and I am not there yet.

Recently, I was reminded of this while talking with a friend whose home flooded during a hurricane. "We are just living day-by-day," she told me. This perfectly echoed my feelings when my own home was damaged in a house fire a few years ago, and we had to move into a short-term apartment rental. There was so much to process and figure out all at once. What phone calls did I need to make? What repairs had to start? Who should we hire to help? Even the most mundane details became daily decisions to consider. How were the kids getting to school? What could we cook with the limited supplies in the kitchen of our temporary apartment? Where did I need to spend the day—at home supervising repairs, at the apartment, or at the office?

I remember telling my coach that my daily life felt like standing waist-deep in heavy surf, struggling to stand up, and being knocked over by wave after wave. "What would you be feeling if you weren't struggling?" she asked. "I'd be relaxed," I said. An image of a life raft appeared in my mind. "I'd be floating. I'd stop fighting the waves and let the water hold me up."

This metaphor was an awakening for me. Ordinarily, I find it challenging to ask for help, and I have plenty of justifications for this: I don't want to burden people, I'm capable of taking care of things myself, and I feel uncomfortable "owing" someone a favor. With the house fire, I was so overwhelmed I had to let all of that go and learn—yet again—how wonderful it is to realize that you are not alone and that many hands are working to hold you up. It was humbling to receive help from so many friends and colleagues. It was even more humbling to realize how much lighter and freer I felt when I learned to accept it graciously.

How does this apply to leading workplace change? One of the unspoken burdens many change leaders carry is a deep sense of responsibility for ensuring everything goes well and according to plan. Because they feel this is a personal duty, they work alone to devise solutions and invest themselves in carrying out their plans. The problem with this tendency is that change is complex. In complex situations, it is often impossible to analyze and plan a response with accuracy. There are too many variables to consider; the situation is fluid and unpredictable. This is especially true when we are dealing with human emotions.

Instead of working alone, trying to design the perfect plan, a better option is to collaborate with others to collect as many viewpoints as possible and then try small things to see what works. We cannot do this effectively working alone. The best way I have found is to let go. When we let go, we open space for others to contribute and for new possibilities to emerge.

NOTICING WHAT EMERGES

Like many people, my first instinct is to resist any change I haven't initiated. After taking time to process my initial reaction, I see possibilities I never would have imagined without the catalyst provided by the change. As the Stoic philosopher Epictetus wrote, "Men are disturbed not by things, but by the views which they take of things" (1890). Once the initial judgment recedes, it is easier to notice and appreciate the benefits and opportunities the change brings.

I find that this is also true when navigating resistance or interacting with "difficult" people while trying to lead change. If we choose to see them as potential teachers, each of these experiences holds lessons for us. The things that trouble us, the patterns that follow us—each lights the path for our learning and growth.

This learning process has revealed some delightful paradoxes for me. When I relax and let go, I feel more grounded and secure. When I accept that I don't know what will happen, I am more prepared to handle whatever comes. Perhaps most surprisingly, when I stop trying so hard, things become much easier.

Conclusion

A Hope for Better Organizational Change

When we face a problem with no clear resolution, when we know that some kind of change is needed, but what specifically needs to be done is unclear, what do we do? Many of us, myself included, try very hard to control what is uncontrollable. We attempt to impose order and clarity where none exists. The more forcefully we do this, the more painful the result.

You can probably recall a time in your career when a leader or coworker attempted to lead change through control. The worst cases exemplify organizational tyranny. A leader imposes an edict that feels arbitrary, illogical, or unfair to provide structure or direction in an ambiguous situation. Resistance follows, and the leader muscularly squashes dissent. The majority moves forward silently, keeping their heads down and their minds elsewhere. Morale plunges, and the situation fails to improve. The leader may have "control" in such a scenario, but the group remains poorly equipped to navigate the change.

In one such experience at a small company many years ago, I recall being awestruck by the difference between two leaders in an extremely tense meeting about a delayed project. We were in the middle of a bidding process for a new software solution. Believing things were taking too long, the enraged CEO called a meeting with several of his direct reports and me, the project manager. He opened the call with a string of expletives, shouting about how incompetent everyone was. "How hard can this be?" he yelled. "We should have had a vendor selected and installed in a week! I could've done it myself in half that time!"

I remember looking on in shock as the tirade continued and then in even greater amazement as one of the VPs calmly responded. "David," she began, "this is a major investment, and it requires time—both for us and the vendors. Most need at least two weeks to respond to our request for proposal." He railed about how ridiculous it was and cursed a few more people by name. Methodically and diplomatically, she explained the current situation and worked toward a productive conclusion. I left the call with tremendous respect for the VP and a conviction to find a new job. (I quit two weeks later.)

Unfortunately, most of us have encountered leaders like this CEO, who use force to respond to uncertainty or difficult situations. This exchange painfully illustrated how poorly he understood the problem. Even worse, it showed that he was unwilling to ask questions or listen to gain understanding. His only tool for managing the situation was his anger.

Most of us have also encountered leaders like the VP, who remain calm and steady regardless of the situation. They focus on the facts, thoughtfully consider the options available, and concentrate on the actions that will keep us moving forward.

He had the title. But she was the leader.

Regardless of our role, each of us has the power to choose how we will respond to change and uncertainty in our organizations. It is easy to underestimate our impact on others, especially if we are not in a formal position of authority. You have more power than you realize.

Consider for a moment what it would be like if all the leaders in your organization chose to respond to change humanely, collaboratively, and productively. Even a few people leading in this way could make a real difference. What would you be able to achieve together?

Could you not be the person who makes that first brave example and begins to light the way?

KEEPING A CLEAN, WELL-LIGHTED PLACE

When I started working on this book, I thought of a short story by Ernest Hemingway that I have held dear for many years. "A Clean, Well-Lighted Place" is set in a Spanish café late at night. A deaf old man sits by himself, drinking brandy. The two waiters are the only others in the café. One is eager to go home; the other is unhurried by the hour. They talk about the man and his failed suicide attempt a week before. Eventually, the old man leaves, and the waiters close up shop. The younger one rushes home to bed; the older one lingers, alone with his thoughts.

What is this story about? Like so much of Hemingway's writing, the most resonant themes are like woodsmoke from a far-off campfire. Unseen but felt, pricking the eyes, tingling the nose.

The older waiter tells his colleague, "Each night I am reluctant to close up because there may be some one who needs the café" (Hemingway 1933, 382). The younger waiter protests that the old man could just as easily drink at home or at another bar. But the older waiter knows this is not the same: "It was the light of course but it is necessary that the place be clean and pleasant" (Hemingway 1933, 382). For him, providing such a space for others is an act of service and compassion. He feels the need for such a space himself.

In our organizations, there are many people who need a clean, well-lighted place, especially as we navigate uncertainty and change. The kind of places most needed allow our loveliest human qualities to emerge: warmth, empathy, clarity, and courage. They encourage quiet and gentle connection, dialogue, and understanding. A clean, well-lighted place is a lamplight in the darkness. It is a welcome warmth reminding us we are human, we matter, and we need not face the unknown alone.

THE COURAGE TO ACT

At the beginning of this book, I shared my beliefs about organizational change. First, change need not be painful for anyone involved. Second, we have a duty to be respectful and humane as we help others through the change process. And third, anyone can lead change in this way.

I sincerely hope that I have convinced you that each of these things is possible and, more importantly, that you can facilitate change in this way. As you've traveled these pages with me, you have gathered perspectives, ideas, and several practical things to try. I also hope the ideas presented here have helped you to appreciate, perhaps in a new way, some wisdom you have always held within yourself.

What matters now is transforming your insights into action. Like the older waiter in the Hemingway story, you can keep a clean, well-lighted place for yourself and others who may need it. The specific techniques you use are far less important than your willingness to listen, your desire to understand, and your courage to act on what you learn.

The courage to act also means the courage to let go. We don't need control to navigate through change confidently. Instead, we need human connection. Connection helps us build a bridge from the present to our unknown future and gives us the courage to cross it together.

Although it is natural to fear the unknown, the unknown also contains wonderful possibilities we might never have imagined. When we take this perspective, we no longer have to protect and shield ourselves against what we do not know. We open ourselves up to new opportunities. We learn to approach the unknown as a traveler might embark on an adventure—full of curiosity, courage, and enthusiasm for what we might find.

Next Steps

Take your learning to the next level by applying the insights you've gained from this book to your own change situation. Start by visiting my website, www.streamsidecoaching.com, or scanning the QR code below to download your free copy of *The Change Leader's Toolkit*. You'll find all the templates and tools mentioned in this book arranged in a printable PDF that you can use for your change effort.

When you sign up for my newsletter, you'll receive the latest information about upcoming community events, workshops, articles, and more resources for thriving with change. I hope to see you at an upcoming event!

If your organization could use help making workplace change more sustainable, respectful, and humane, please contact me at michelle@streamsidecoaching.com. I'd love to support you in creating your own clean, well-lighted places for change to flourish.

Acknowledgments

I am deeply grateful to the many people who have helped and inspired me throughout the process of writing this book.

First, thank you to my clients for trusting me with your business and inviting me to help. This work would not exist without you.

Thank you to my early readers, who shared feedback on early drafts of the manuscript and helped me to refine and polish my ideas, including Meg Severino, Tanner Wortham, Alexandria Keith, Shannon McCue, and several other family members and friends. I owe a special debt of gratitude to Victor Pena, my colleague and friend, who tirelessly listened to my ideas for more than a year and offered detailed suggestions that vastly improved the final product.

Many thanks to my publishing team for lending their considerable talents to bring this book to life: Liz Wheeler for her careful and elegant editing, Mary Jo Slazak Courchesne for her thorough permissions research, and Elisabeth Heissler for her gorgeous cover and interior design.

Thank you to the wonderful coaching faculty at the University of Texas at Dallas Naveen Jindal School of Management, who introduced me to many of the psychological concepts referenced in this book. I am also grateful to my coaching buddies, Marguerite Thibodeaux and June Horie, who helped me apply these ideas as we refined our coaching skills together, and who continue to support me through our regular chats.

Thank you to my talented colleagues and past leaders, who have listened to my ideas, influenced my thinking, and helped me to grow. I am especially grateful to the Agile coaching communities I've participated in, and to the many software teams I've had the privilege to learn from throughout the years.

I am fortunate to have had the opportunity to learn from several brilliant leaders in the Agile field and have appreciated their mentorship and example. Thank you to Bob Galen, Bill Joiner, Debra Whitestone, Mary Thorn, Debbie Wallace, Jennifer Fields, Matt Philip, Jon Smart, and Don MacIntyre for providing inspiration, guidance, and encouragement.

Throughout the process of writing this book, I have benefited from excellent coaching from Pam Aks, my former teacher and brilliant mindset coach, and Connie Whitesell, my incredibly thoughtful and supportive business coach. This process would have been infinitely harder without their help.

Most of all, thank you to my family for your boundless love and support: my parents, Roger Pauk and Diane Pauk; my step-parents, Jean Pauk and Dan Hall; my sisters, Danielle Pauk and Stephanie Mattucci; my incredible husband, Derik Hinz; and my delightful children, Ingrid and Owen. Thank you for keeping a clean, well-lighted place in your hearts, where I always feel at home.

References

Aurelius, Marcus and George Long. 1882. *Meditations of Marcus Aurelius Antoninus, emperor of the Romans.* C. H. Shaver. PDF. https://www.loc.gov/item/27007869/. Accessed on April 22, 2025.

Coutu, Diane. 2002. "The Anxiety of Learning." *Harvard Business Review*, March. https://hbr.org/2002/03/the-anxiety-of-learning.

Epictetus. 1890. *The Works of Epictetus: His Discourses, in Four Books, the Enchiridion, and Fragments.* Translated by Thomas Wentworth Higginson. Thomas Nelson and Sons. http://data.perseus.org/citations/urn:cts:greekLit:tlg0557.tlg002.perseus-eng2:5. Accessed on April 22, 2025.

Hemingway, Ernest. 1995. "A Clean, Well-Lighted Place." In *The Short Stories*. Simon & Schuster Inc.

Hicks, Robert F. 2017. *The Process of Highly Effective Coaching: An Evidence-Based Framework.* Taylor & Francis.

Kotter, John P. 2007. "Leading Change: Why Transformation Efforts Fail." *Harvard Business Review*, January. https://hbr.org/1995/05/leading-change-why-transformation-efforts-fail-2.

Ladau, Emily. 2022. "Tweet." January 5. https://x.com/emily_ladau/status/1478566115114725380?lang=en.

Lewin, Kurt. 1936. *Principles of Topological Psychology.* McGraw-Hill.

Liberating Structures. "1-1-2-4-All." https://www.liberatingstructures.com/1-1-2-4-all/. Accessed on April 9, 2025.

Miller, William, and Stephen Rollnick. 2013. *Motivational Interviewing: Helping People Change.* 3rd ed. The Guilford Press.

Orem, Sara L., Jacqueline Binkert, and Ann L. Clancy. 2007. *Appreciative Coaching: A Positive Process for Change.* Jossey-Bass.

Satir, Virginia, et al. 1991. *The Satir Model: Family Therapy and Beyond.* Science and Behavior Books, Inc.

Schein, Edgar H. 2013. *Humble Inquiry: The Gentle Art of Asking Instead of Telling.* Berrett-Koehler Publishers, Inc.

Credits

I wish to thank the authors, publishers, and copyright holders listed below for their generosity in granting permission to reprint passages from their works. This book has been enriched by their contributions.

From *The Process of Highly Effective Coaching: An Evidence-Based Framework* by Robert F. Hicks. Copyright © 2017 Robert F. Hicks. Used with permission of Taylor & Francis Group, LLC; permission conveyed through Copyright Clearance Center, Inc.

From *Humble Inquiry: The Gentle Art of Asking Instead of Telling* by Edgar H. Schein. Copyright © 2013 Edgar H. Schein. Used with permission of Berrett-Koehler Publishers, Inc.; permission conveyed through Copyright Clearance Center, Inc.

From *Liberating Structures*, "1-1-2-4-All," by Keith McCandless and Henri Lipmanowicz. Licensed by Creative Commons License Attribution-Non-Commercial Unported 3.0. Reprinted with permission of co-author Keith McCandless.

From *Harvard Business Review*, "The Anxiety of Learning" by Diane Coutu. Published March 2002. Copyright © 2002 Harvard Business School Publishing Corporation. Reprinted with permission of the publisher.

From *The Satir Model: Family Therapy and Beyond*, by Virginia Satir, John Banmen, Jane Gerber, and Maria Gomori. Copyright © 1991 Science and Behavior Books, Inc. Reprinted with permission of co-author Dr. John Banmen.

From *Harvard Business Review*, "Leading Change: Why Transformation Efforts Fail" by John P. Kotter. Published January 2007.

Recommended Further Reading

Avery, Christopher M., Meri Aaron Walker, and Erin O'Toole Murphy. 2001. *Teamwork Is an Individual Skill: Getting Your Work Done When Sharing Responsibility*. Berrett-Koehler Publishers, Inc. Kindle edition.

Berne, Eric. 2016. *Games People Play: The Psychology of Human Relationships*. Penguin Random House UK.

Burns, David D. M.D. 1999. *The Feeling Good Handbook*. Plume.

Edmondson, Amy C. 2018. *The Fearless Organization: Creating Psychological Safety in the Workplace for Learning, Innovation, and Growth*. John Wiley & Sons.

Hackman, J. Richard. 2002. *Leading Teams: Setting the Stage for Great Performances*. Harvard Business Review Press.

Joiner, Bill, and Stephen Josephs. 2006. *Leadership Agility: Five Levels of Mastery for Anticipating and Initiating Change*. Jossey-Bass.

Liker, Jeffrey K. 2003. *The Toyota Way: 14 Management Principles from the World's Greatest Manufacturer*. McGraw-Hill. Kindle edition.

Rock, David. 2008. "SCARF: A Brain-Based Model for Collaborating with and Influencing Others." *NeuroLeadership Journal* 1. https://schoolguide.casel.org/uploads/sites/2/2018/12/SCARF-NeuroleadershipArticle.pdf

Schein, Edgar H. 2016. *Organizational Culture and Leadership*. 5th ed. Wiley.

Seligman, Martin. 2011. *Flourish: A Visionary New Understanding of Happiness and Well-being*. Free Press.

Snowden, David J., and Mary E. Boone. 2007. "A Leader's Framework for Decision Making." *Harvard Business Review*, November. https://hbr.org/2007/11/a-leaders-framework-for-decision-making.

Ury, William. 1993. *Getting Past No: Negotiating in Difficult Situations*. Bantam.

About the Author

Michelle Pauk is the founder of Streamside Coaching, a coaching and consulting firm dedicated to helping organizations lead change and build collaborative cultures. Her clients include executives and change agents at Fortune 100s, non-profits, and fast-growing startups. A Professional Certified Coach with the International Coaching Federation, she holds a master's in leadership and organizational development. She lives in Tennessee with her husband and two children. You can connect with Michelle on LinkedIn at www.linkedin.com/in/michelle-pauk, or reach her via email at michelle@streamsidecoaching.com.

www.ingramcontent.com/pod-product-compliance
Lightning Source LLC
Chambersburg PA
CBHW030525210326
41597CB00013B/1032